MW00582904

RECLAIMING OURSELVES

EMMA KATHRYN

RECLAIMING OURSELVES

EMMA KATHRYN

This work CC-BY-NC-SA 2020 by Emma Kathryn

All reproductions must be for non-commercial use only, must bear attribution to the author, and must carry this same license.

ISNB: 978-1-7357944-1-9

Gods&Radicals Press
an imprint of RITONA a.s.b.l
3 Rue de Wormeldange
Rodenbourg, Luxembourg
L-1695

Editorial, Layout, and Design: Rhyd Wildermuth
Cover Image: CC-O Miriam Espacio va Unsplash.com

View our catalogue and online journal at
ABEAUTIFULRESISTANCE.ORG

Contents

INTRODUCTION

We live in a world that is not of our own making.

Or perhaps that is not quite right, for haven't we all contributed to this system? Aren't we all but cogs in the machine?

We are born into this system of capitalism, a global system, raised within it and trained to become a working, unthinking part of it until we die in it, and then we are soon forgotten: for the wheel of capitalism keeps turning, rolling over all in its wake.

We are more than unthinking, unfeeling machines. We are more than this man-made world of capitalism, and many are beginning to wake up to this truth. But what good is an awakening if we are unable to free ourselves from that which binds us?

This short book is aimed at those who have gone through the process of realisation. For many this is a long process—it doesn't happen overnight. Instead, it occurs incrementally, bit by bit. At first it may start off as a yearning for something deeper, and many find solace in the cure capitalism offers in the form of self-help or other neatly packaged escapism, never moving on from this step. But some of us soon realise the trap for what it is and seek other—more useful—ways of becoming free.

Capitalism has become so pervasive that the majority no longer know how to live outside of it. This book then is for those of us who want to take the first steps in learning to live outside of its confines. It contains nothing particularly new, but rather some old-fashioned ideas about becoming less reliant on the system and more reliant on ourselves.

How many of us would survive if governments collapsed or withdrew their blanket of convenience to which we have all become so accustomed? Such things become luxuries that dull our senses and dumb us down: the system would hold less power over us if we weren't dependent on it for our survival.

How many of us could successfully grow, forage, or hunt for enough food to feed ourselves, our families, and our communities? How many could help cure or ease the symptoms of common ailments for which we've become over reliant on Big Pharma? And it goes on and on: capitalism has taken over every aspect of living, so that we have become so completely reliant upon it.

This small book aims to redress the balance. The skills and knowledge contained herein will not lead to overnight rebellion and a quick collapse of the system, but rather will allow us to reclaim ourselves, even if only a little. Do not be disheartened: all resistance and rebellion starts as a trickle, it's just that many don't notice until that trickle grows into a raging river that sweeps away everything in its path.

The aim of this book is to give us the basic tools of freedom, tools that we can build upon as we progress and learn skills that can free us from the fear that rising up against a system designed to keep us down might bring, the fear of having enough to eat, the fear of being unable to live.

And so let us begin on this journey of self reclamation, for you have found yourselves here for your own reasons and do not need me to explain them to you. As we develop and strengthen ourselves, we will also develop the basic skills found here and in doing so act as a beacon for others who may wish to follow suit. At the very least they will allow you to live a little more freely. How far you take things after is up to you, but you might just surprise yourself, you might find that the waters of rebellion and of resistance run deep within you.

RECLAIMING FOOD

We begin the reclaiming process with food, or more specifically with the sourcing of food, its production, preparations, and cooking. We start here with good reason.

Food is perhaps the easiest and most obvious way in which we have been and continue to be controlled and oppressed. Those of us who have ever gone truly hungry will know just how debilitating it can be, emotionally, psychologically, and physically. And the fear of not being able to feed ourselves and those reliant upon us, our families and our children is just as damaging. To face that pressure day in and day out is intolerable, and when you find yourself in that situation, it's all you can think about.

What was once a struggle for the very poorest in our society now affects even those who might once have been considered middle class, at least the lower end of that field. Now even in wealthy countries there is a rise in people who work full time who must rely on charity to feed themselves. In the U.K. there are more food banks than there are McDonald's. And for those who have always been at the bottom of society, well, things always find a way of getting worse, even when you think they can't possibly.

If we are unable to feed ourselves—the most basic of our needs—then how can we hope to fight against the capitalist system that keeps us all enslaved? If our time and effort is taken up working jobs that don't even pay enough to survive, with the threat of being unable to feed ourselves keeping us quiet and subservient, then how can we ever hope to have the time and energy to fight back?

Reclaiming food must be the first step in the process of reclaiming ourselves. The good news is that, just as it is the easiest way of oppressing us, it is the easiest way in which we can free ourselves. We can take direct action and, believe me, action will be needed. We will have to put in the graft. We must learn new skills and relearn those that we have forgotten or have been made to forget. We must forgo the convenience of convenience and master the skills and knowledge of those who came before us. We must learn how to grow, forage, hunt, and cook and we must relearn these vital skills now. We must become proficient in them before we need them.

As I've already said, there is work to be done and not everyone will be able to do everything, or indeed want to. As I always say, take what works for you and discard the rest (and it's here our community and solidarity links come into play). So let us begin the work of reclaiming food.

RECLAIMING FOOD RIGHT NOW

Reclaiming food right now is often an issue that gets overlooked. Sure, growing, foraging, and hunting are extremely important skills that will provide us with fresh and truly sustainable food and we will cover them later on. But what about right now, right this minute? We must keep in mind that so many people will be starting from a place of deprivation. Growing, harvesting, hunting, and foraging are all important tasks but they are also require huge amounts of energy, effort, and time if they are to provide all or most of what we require. Exploring how we get our food right now is vitally important both in terms of being able to eat properly and how we prepare what is available to us in the best possible way to get maximum nutrition and to make it go further.

The first task then is to look at how much food we use over the course of a day and then how much we use weekly.

Exercise

Keeping a food diary can often sound like a frivolous task and before I used to fight in the kickboxing and boxing ring, I thought so too. They are, however, an extremely useful tool to gauge not only what you're eating and drinking but also how much.

This exercise then is keeping record for the purpose of analysis. Keep a food diary for a week, always being completely honest (and why not, this isn't a diet!). This will give you a complete picture of how much food you are consuming as well as an idea into the kinds of foods you are eating.

At the same time as keeping a food diary, I would also like you to record how much you are spending on food and how much of that food then gets thrown away unused.

At the end of the week, go through your food diary and spending record. This will help highlight any discrepancies between spending, eating, and any food wastage. Most people overspend on their food and show food wastage at home. It's one of those things that is easily done, largely because sourcing food and eating it have become separate activities.

Even the most vigilant of us finds that there is some food wastage in the home. Part of it is that so many of us are forced into working long hours in exhausting jobs and, at the end of the week or on payday, we file down to the local supermarket and buy what we might need for the coming week in advance. In my own experiences early on, I'd have the best of intentions, filling my trolley with all kinds of fresh delights with the intention of cooking glorious dishes from scratch only to find that after finishing work each day I was too tired to and so convenience food would do. So much of that food ended up in the bin. In that instant of coming home from work exhausted, it's all too easy to call for a takeaway or pop some ready meals into the oven. It's a rut many people find themselves in and one that's easy to stay in.

This exercise gives you a clear snapshot of how much you are buying and how much you are consuming. It is also important for later on, as it gives a valuable insight into how much food you will need to source in order to be comfortable.

Exercise

Now it's time to look at where your food is coming from, and by that, I mean how you are procuring the food you eat now. As I've already mentioned, this is important because we must start our reclaiming process somewhere. Most of us will be starting from a place firmly within the capitalist structure; that is, buying our food from supermarkets and shops. For the vast majority of us, particularly in Western, industrialised countries, there is very little choice. We have become almost naturalised to it.

So to begin, make a list of all the places where you currently get your food from, whether that be supermarkets, the local market, farmers markets, etc.. Next, note your reasons for shopping there. Is it closest, or perhaps a stop off point after a busy day at work? Is it cheap prices that keep you going back? Whatever your reasoning, this exercise allows you to notice any recurring patterns, to make you more aware of the thought processes behind your habits, something so many of us rarely consider.

Both of these exercises will give you a clear picture of not only your eating habits but also clear insight into some of the often unconscious behaviors that reinforce and affect our food buying, consumption, and wastage.

Exploring and understanding what we are doing now will ultimately allow us to start to climb out of the ruts we find ourselves in.

Shopping for Food

Hand in hand with food wastage goes struggling to afford food in the first place, which in turn fuels unhealthy eating habits that can contribute to obesity and illnesses such as type 2 diabetes. Being unable to afford fresh whole foods means that people come to rely on heavily processed, frozen, and fried foods which, when eaten over time, can lead to significant reductions in health and wellbeing.

Eating well doesn't have to cost loads of money, though sometimes it can feel this way. As well as cooking from scratch, knowing where to shop for your food now can also see significant reductions in how much money you're spending on groceries.

Discount Stores

Even though my town is quite small, it still has two of the famous European low cost supermarkets. These alone can help massively when it comes to reducing money spent on food. Yet there is still an element of food snobbery, in that despite the good quality of the food, many still have an aversion to shopping off-brand. The fact that some people still turn their noses up because the cost is significantly lower is pure craziness. Even in supermarkets such as these there are still plenty of offers and reductions, especially for food with low use-by dates.

Markets

I live in a market town in the middle of England, complete with red and white striped stalls and a cobblestone market square. How quaint! But imagery aside, the market is one of the best places to buy fresh food, vegetables, fruit, fish, and meat. Not only are the stall holders local people, but so is the food. The food is often cheaper than supermarkets because of the reduced costs involved and many local traders give their regular customers discounts. Plus if you are able to, if you can time your visit to the market later on in the afternoon, then the prices are slashed further to encourage quick sales as the traders need to clear their days' produce. Then there are folks who wait until the market traders leave as they leave behind fruit and vegetables that are still good, but perhaps will not be in sellable condition the next day. They leave these on the stalls in cardboard boxes for people to take. Even if the left-overs are not quite at their best, for example soft or bruised fruit, these are perfect for cooking with. I've never understood why cookbooks tell you to use the freshest ingredients for things like apple pies or jams, as traditionally these are the foods that would have been destined for the cooker whilst the fresh stuff would be for eating straight away, fresh from the basket.

Other

Now admittedly, this option will not be to everyone's taste but I know folks who will also go dumpster diving. The local corner shop owned by local shopkeepers are quickly becoming a thing of the past. Supermarkets are opening smaller express shops, springing up in every neighborhood, and local shopkeepers just cannot compete with the buying and advertising might of these corporations.

Yet these business models are so very wasteful. My partner is a delivery driver for a local bakery who supplies some of these types of shops, and he's always telling me about the masses of food they throw away, food with nothing wrong with it. The problem is that stock is always coming, whether the shops need it or not, and so they end up throwing away huge amounts of fresh food.

There are people who will take advantage of this foolishness and will take it from the food waste dumpsters. The food itself is often packaged to the hilt and is in good condition, so why not?

Storing Food

How to store your food is key in reducing food wastage and ultimately how much money you spend on it. For foods with a long shelf life or that are of the freshest calibre, then that's easy enough, but knowing what to do with things with a low use-by date can be a challenge. Here are some suggestions, all of which I use at home.

Cooking: by cooking the food, making meals that can be refrigerated for up to two days or frozen for up to a week or two, you can make your food last longer with the benefit of having good meals that require no more preparation than reheating. This is perfect for those of us who work long hours, and reduces the reliance on store bought ready-meals and takeaways.

Freezing: you can freeze foods with a low use-by date, though some fruits do not freeze well, such as strawberries, which is fine for those foods that will end up in sauces, smoothies, or other dishes that change the texture of the food anyway.

Other: making preserves and sauces are another way of extending the shelf life of your fresh produce. Pickling is good for vegetables and fruit leathers make a tasty sweet treat that is a nice alternative to jams. Making candied fruit rinds is a great way of using up citrus fruit peel.

Cooking

Cooking meals from scratch using whole foods is a great way of making our food and our money last longer and go further. You'd be forgiven for thinking otherwise: it's been drummed into us by the media that processed food is cheaper, and when you go shopping, it's easy to believe it when you are confronted with the price of a frozen ready-meal versus the cost of ingredients to make the same meal from fresh food.

Yet this is a fallacy when you consider portion amounts and the fact that the ingredients bought will also be used in other meals. But for the person who is strapped for cash and time, when at their supermarket of convenience, such thoughts are often far from their minds. In this way and a myriad of others, we have become separated from all aspects of food, from its production right through to cooking and consuming.

The recipes included here are all the ones I use at home and are mostly simple but delicious. You'll also notice that there is room for any number of substitutions to account for diet choices. Some of the recipes are the basis for many everyday meals and can be made in advance and kept frozen or refrigerated to save time and effort. Like most things in life, once you've got the hang of these basics, other meals and cooking techniques will naturally follow.

Stocks

Stocks are an important cooking skill to master as they form the basis of many meals.

Now I will add a quick note here. Eating meat is one of those issues that is becoming more controversial and contentious. All stocks with the exception of vegetable stock are made using bones. Whatever your views on eating meat (I myself am a vegetarian whereas my family all eat meat), these recipes are important to at least look at. And if you or your family do eat meat, using the leftover bones for stock is just another way of making your money and food go further. And seeing as how we are on the topic of meat, let's start with meat stocks.

Very simply then, meat stocks involve boiling the bones in a large pot of water until the liquid reduces and you're left with a thick, soupy liquid. The boiling of the bones does two things. First, especially in the case of using a roast chicken carcass, the process strips those little pieces of meat from the bones, and second, it releases the marrow from the bones. I basically use the same recipe for whatever meat bones I have available.

Meat Stock

You will need:
- A pot large enough for the bones
- The bones or carcass
- A head of garlic depending on taste, crushed by the end of your knife or palm of your hand
- 2-3 sticks of celery, roughly chopped
- 2-3 carrots, roughly chopped
- 3 onions, quartered
- Herbs (and here feel free to use any you have available or those you simply like the taste of though I always add a bay leaf or two).

These are so easy to make. Simply place all of the ingredients into your pan and fill with water so that the bones are covered. Place on the heat and bring to the boil before turning down the heat and let it simmer. Leave for around an hour or until the liquid has reduced by half, then simply strain into a clean container and allow to cool. When it has cooled, you'll notice that the fat has solidified and this can be scraped off. You may also find that the stock itself has become jelly-like and this is totally acceptable.

Bone Broth

For a simple broth, follow the recipe above but instead of leaving it to cool and solidify, drain the liquid into a clean pan and add potatoes and whatever vegetables you like. Return to the heat until the potatoes are soft and there you have it, a simple but nutritious broth that costs next to nothing to make. You can eat straight away, keep in the fridge for up to two days or freeze for up to six months.

Fish Stock / Shellfish Stock

You will need:
• Fish bones and tails, shrimp shells, crab shell, lobster shells, etc. Please stay clear of gills and guts when it comes to using seafood leftovers.
  • 2 onions, quartered
  • 2 garlic cloves
  • 2 carrots roughly chopped
  • 2 sticks of celery, roughly chopped
  • 2 bay leaves
  • A sprig of rosemary
  • A handful of parsley
  • Optional: 1 cup of white wine
  • Optional: 10 peppercorns.

Simply follow the same method for the meat stock and store the same way. You can use the stock in rice dishes such as risotto or as the basis for pasta sauces to be eaten with fish or to make a roux for fish pie.

Vegetable Stock

I use all of my vegetable scraps to make this, such as carrot and onion ends. I simply freeze them until needed.

In a large pan add your veg scraps and if needed add:
- 2-3 chopped onions
- 3 carrots, roughly chopped
- At least 3 cloves of garlic (I like garlic so use more, but you can adjust to suit your own tastes)
- 2-3 sticks of celery
- 2 sprigs of thyme
- 2 sprigs of rosemary
- 2 bay leaves

Cover with water and bring to the boil before allowing to simmer for around an hour or until the liquid has reduced by half. Strain and use straight away, refrigerate for up to 2 days or freeze for up to 6 months.

Vegetable Soup

You will need:
- 2 onions
- 2 leeks
- 1 or 2 garlic cloves
- 2 carrots

- 1 celery stick
- Potatoes
- Vegetable stock
- 2 tablespoons of butter
- 2 tablespoons of flour
- 300ml of water (more depending on how much liquid stock you have)

In a large pan, melt the butter over a medium heat. Chop the onion, leeks, and celery and sauté until soft, adding chopped garlic. Add the flour and mix in before slowly adding the vegetable stock, continuously stirring until the liquid is smooth and the flour dissolved. Next add the rest of the vegetables and potatoes and allow to simmer until the vegetables are cooked through and soft. Add salt and pepper to taste.

Soups are easy, cheap and delicious and can be saved in the fridge or frozen. Vegetable soups can also be made using chicken stock, and the beauty of soups is that they all follow a basic methodology thus allowing you to adapt recipes to suit the ingredients you have available.

Stews and Casseroles

Stews and casseroles are a natural progression from soups and are some of my favorite things to cook. Not only are they hearty and substantial, but you can use seasonal ingredients, making them apt for any time of year. They are also relatively cheap to make, and if you eat meat you can use cheaper cuts as the slower cooking time means that meat is soft and tender. And, if like me, you do not eat meat then you can use any vegetables you like!

There is little difference between stews and casseroles. You can use exactly the same ingredients for both, but what makes them different is the cooking method. Casseroles are generally cooked in the oven, whilst stews are cooked on the stove top. These dishes are easy to cook and everything can be placed in a large pot and cooked together. A slow cooker adds to the ease of these dishes and is especially useful for those who work long hours. It means they can come home to a healthy cooked meal without having to do little more than dish it up.

My basic casserole / stew recipe is one I use all the time at home. Simply substitute those ingredients you don't like, using a suitable stock.

You will need:

• 2 onions and chopped
• 2 cloves of garlic, finely cut
• Stock of choice—meat stock for casseroles and stews containing meat, and vegetable or chicken stock for vegetable casseroles
• 3 carrots, sliced
• Meat of choice, chopped (for vegetable dishes, just leave the meat out).
• 2 sticks of celery, chopped
• Any other seasonal vegetables.

If you don't have much time for preparation or you are making a casserole, simply place all of the ingredients into a large casserole dish, pop the lid on and place in the oven at around 150 degrees celsius (300 degrees fahrenheit) for around 2-3 hours. If using a slow cooker, place all the ingredients into the crock pot and turn to low. Leave for around 5 hours or until you get home from work or wherever else you are going.

If cooking on the stove top, add a little oil to the pot and brown the meat, adding the onions, celery and garlic until soft. Add the rest of your ingredients and turn to a low setting. Cover and allow to simmer, stirring occasionally until the meat is soft and tender.

You can serve with potatoes or add potatoes to the pot so that you have a decent one pot meal. Dumplings are a tasty extra to add and are simply made using self raising flour, suet or butter, and water, seasoning with salt and herbs. Mix the ingredients together until you have a sticky dough and add to the pot during the last half an hour of cooking.

Any leftovers can be kept in the fridge for up to two days or frozen for around 2 months.

Gravies and Sauces

Gravies and sauces are really quite simple to make and once you've got the basics down you can make any sauce you want.

One way of making gravies is quite common and one most people are used to. After roasting meat, remove the meat from the tray and place on the stove top. Add water to the juices and really mix together well. Add flour to thicken.

You can also take the stocks from the recipes above and use flour to thicken these too.

Learning how to make a basic white sauce can really add a lot of variety to your meals and often forms the base for so many other sauces including parsley sauce, onion sauce, cheese sauce and so on.

For a basic white sauce, you will need:

- 50g (2 oz) butter
- 50g (2 oz) flour
- 500ml (18 fl oz) milk

Melt the butter over a medium heat and add the flour to the pan, stirring constantly. Don't be alarmed if it forms a paste, it's supposed to. Stir for a minute as this allows the raw flour to cook out and then add the milk a little at a time, whisking constantly. You should see the lumps begin to dissolve until you have a thick velvety sauce. This is a very basic sauce but you can jazz it up a little.

You will need:

- 1 onion finely chopped
- 2 garlic cloves, finely chopped or grated
- 50g (2 oz) butter
- 50g (2 oz) flour
- 500ml (18 fl oz) milk

Melt the butter in a pan and saute the onions and garlic until soft. Add the flour and mix it in making sure it doesn't stick to the bottom. At this stage the mixture looks clumpy but this is okay! Slowly add the milk, always mixing it in until the flour has dissolved and you have a silky smooth sauce. You can add water, stock or more milk to achieve the consistency you require, along with any other herbs or ingredients.

You can use this sauce for pie fillings as well. I love to make a vegetable pie using up any leftover cooked vegetable. Just add the vegetables to the sauce and encase in a shortcrust pastry.

Bread

I love bread! Despite it being somewhat demonised in modern healthy eating fads, bread is a staple for many people around the world. It is cheap to make and filling, and if you've got bread in the cupboard then you have the basis for many meals. Many people today have bread makers in the home, but this very basic recipe requires nothing more than the ingredients, an oven, and some elbow grease!

You will need:
- 500g (18 oz) of strong plain flour
- 7g (0.3 oz) of dried yeast or 5g of fresh yeast
- 30ml (1 fl oz)of water
- 25g (1 oz) of butter or 3 tablespoons of oil

If using fresh yeast then you will have to prepare it before use. Simply place in a dish and break it up using a fork. For both dry and fresh yeast, add to a little warm (just under body temperature) water and leave for 5 or 10 minutes. The yeast should start to bubble or foam.

Sieve the dry ingredients into a large mixing bowl. Make a well in the centre and add the oil, water, and yeast mixture and bring together to form a dough. Tip it onto a lightly floured surface and knead for at least 10 minutes before returning back to the bowl. Cover with a damp tea towel and place somewhere warm for around 45 minutes or until the dough has doubled in size. Some people like to knead the dough again at this point before shaping or placing in a loaf tin. Bake at around 200 degrees celsius until it is golden brown and sounds hollow when tapped. Leave to cool.

Baked egg toast

This recipe is so simple and yet so delicious! It makes a very good lunch or serve with a seasonal salad for a larger meal.

You will need:
- A slice of bread
- An egg
- Grated cheese

Place a slice of bread on a baking tray and use the back of a spoon to flatten the bread in the centre, making a well. Crack the egg in the well and sprinkle grated cheese around the edges. Bake in the oven at around 180 degrees celsius (350 fahrenheit) until the egg is cooked. Season with a little black pepper.

Soda Bread

Soda bread is great if you don't have any yeast to hand and is one of my favorite breads. It is easy and quick to make, requiring no proofing time and no heavy kneading.

You will need:
- 300g (11 oz) plain flour
- 1 level teaspoon of bicarbonate of soda
- 250ml (9 fl oz) of water.

Simply sieve the dry ingredients into a mixing bowl before making a well in the centre. Add the water and mix until you have a dough. Turn out onto a lightly floured surface and knead lightly before shaping into a ball. Place onto a baking tray and flatten slightly. Then, using a sharp knife, cut a cross into the top before placing in a hot oven and bake at 200 degrees celsius until golden brown.

Pastry

This is a recipe for a very basic shortcrust pastry and I've included it instead of other types of pastry for two reasons. It is very versatile and is great in savory and sweet dishes (for sweet things add sugar to taste or 100g for this recipe). Secondly, it is very easy and cheap to make.

You will need:
- 300g (11 oz) of plain flour
- 150g (5 oz) butter, cubed
- 3 tbsp of water to bind
- A pinch of salt
- 100g (4 oz) sugar for a sweetened pastry

Sieve the dry ingredients into a large mixing bowl and add the butter, using your fingertips to mix the butter into the flour so that it resembles crumbs. Add the water and bring the mixture together to form a dough. Roll out as desired on a floured surface.

You can jazz this very basic pastry up by adding herbs and other seasonings to taste. One of my favorite things is to add grated cheese and chili flakes and roll out, using a cutter to make savory biscuits! You can make pies by using any left over stews and casseroles and encasing them in the pastry for a filling and delicious meal.

Foraging

I adore foraging, and the truth is I am out doing it all year round. 'Nature provides' or so the saying tells us, and it is very true. Whilst summer and autumn are the heavy hitters when it comes to quantity and variety, for those with a keen eye and knowledge of their local landscape, winter and early spring still have fresh goodies to offer.

But before you can get any good from the land, you need to get out and about and familiarize yourself with your environment. Now, it is true that those who, like myself, live in more rural areas will find plentiful supplies of fresh foods, even those in more urban areas and even cities will find some. Getting to know the lay of the land is an important part of this. We will look at this in greater detail later on, but for now making the effort to go out and really pay attention to what grows around you is all that is needed in order to forage successfully.

Foraging is one of those practices where the more you get out, the more you will learn and thus the more you will gather. Getting out at least once a week is vital. If you are totally new to foraging, then these first weekly forays will be something of a scouting exercise, paying attention to what grows and where. As you go, try and identify some of the plants and trees you come across. As you progress on your journey, you will also notice other things, such as the micro-climates of different places which affect what grows there and when. For instance the elder trees in my garden always flower about two weeks before the trees in a field no more than a two minute walk from home, and the same goes for the berries, too. Getting out and learning to look at where you live with new eyes is the first step in beginning your foraging journey.

Exercise

So now it's time to go and explore!

Make sure you dress not only for the weather, but for the terrain as well. If in doubt, a good pair of walking shoes will serve you well. If the weather is dry and the area is not too wild, trainers will do it. I'm a fan of making use of what you already have, a throwback from the not-too distant past where I couldn't afford to buy anything extra, nevermind specialist footwear or clothes. I can't tell you the number of times I was put off doing some activity or other because a so-called expert would say buy the best equipment you can afford. The truth is I couldn't afford anything! So do not let not having such things deter you. It may well be that as you progress on your own journey, whatever that may be, you will find the resources to get the items that were once a luxury you could ill afford. I will say when you are out, particularly in remote areas, be careful—if the terrain doesn't suit your footwear or clothing, then use your common sense and proceed with care.

This exercise can be done no matter where you live, be it town, city, or open countryside. The point is you begin to form a working relationship with the land. Make an effort to get out weekly to really see the changes that occur where you live. You don't need to cover miles and miles in one go, but instead explore small patches of your local landscape. You might find yourself drawn to certain places in your neighborhood, but if you are unsure, if there's a park or field near where you live, start there. Go for a walk and really pay attention to what grows there. Try to identify as many of the plants and trees as you can, and you'll soon see the wide variety of species that grow there. You will be surprised at how much you never noticed about your local spaces.

Make an effort to also go out at different times of the day. Notice sunlight patterns and those places that get early morning light, the late afternoon sun, or are in full sun all day. You will become familiar with local rainfall patterns, those places that gather water, areas that are more open and those that are sheltered. All of these factors will affect what types of plants and trees will grow and thrive in these areas. Whilst it is amazingly good for body and soul to get out in nature, try and treat these excursions as learning sessions. Take a notebook, something small you can scribble or sketch in.

Whilst many would-be foragers skip this step, eager to find any edible delights, for those who are serious about foraging, about finding sustenance from the wild, I would urge you to stick with it. Such exercises will give you a solid base from which to expand. Once you are used to looking at your local area in a critical way, you will be able to use that knowledge in unknown areas, learning to read the signs and symbols of nature. As with most things in life, the basics remain the same and the knowledge from your own locality can be applied to new areas.

Identifying Plants

As you continue to explore your local landscape you will begin to notice in ever growing detail the plants and trees that grow there. There will be the common plants that you are familiar with such as dandelions and daisies, but there will be loads of plants you don't know. And that's a good thing!

Now I will say that this section is not going to be a plant identification guide. There are plenty of good ones out there already, and I would urge you to check out second-hand book shops, charity shops, and flea markets. Choose one with clear pictures and ideally those that look at different parts of the plant. There are also lots of websites you can use as well as free apps where you can take a picture of a plant and the app searches for it in its databases. These are useful, but make sure you don't become over reliant on them as they do have a tendency to make the best of us lazy. Besides, once you've learned to identify a plant yourself you won't forget it quickly.

The correct identification of plants is extremely important for your own health and safety, especially when looking for edible foods. For example, if you take a plant such as yarrow or even elder, there are several types of plant that can be mistaken for them. Both have sprays of tiny white flowers, but so too do poison hemlock and hogweed, both of which are highly poisonous and will cause damage. Hogweed will leave you with severe burns if you happen to get the sap on your skin, and poison hemlock can kill or leave you hospitalized. With that said then, you must learn to recognize several features of certain plants to help keep you safe. For example, poison hemlock does look very similar to yarrow but has a purplish stem and hogweed is a very large plant, much bigger than yarrow.

Flowers: These are perhaps the biggest clues when it comes to plant identification. When considering flowers, there are a few things to look out for. The obvious clue is the color of the flowers with the size of the flower heads being another one. You will also need to consider petal shape, size and arrangement as well as the quantity.

Leaves: As with flowers there is much we can tell from the leaves of a plant or tree. The flowering time for many plants and trees is often limited, whereas the leaves will be present during the spring, summer, and autumn. With this in mind then, it is well worth learning how to identify plants and trees using their leaves. As with flowers, the size and shape of the leaf can be one of the biggest indicators of species, particularly if the leaves are distinctive. You will also want to look at how they are attached to the plant. Are they attached directly to the stem or do they have a stalk? How are the leaves arranged? Are they arranged in opposites or whorls? Consider the leaf margins (the edges of the leaf). Are they smooth or serrated and does it continue around the whole leaf?

Trees: When it comes to trees, of course use any flowers and the leaves to help in the identification process but bark can be a big giveaway. Is it smooth or rough and are there any ridges or other distinctive markings? What about the color of the bark, and how does it feel? Is it smooth or papery? With trees, also consider the height of the tree and the spread of the branches.

Location: Some plants will thrive almost anywhere, but most have specific needs, so the location of a plant can be used in conjunction with the other pointers given to narrow down the possibilities. Consider the light to shade ratio and how wet or dry the area is, as well as soil type.

Use all of the above to help you identify plants and trees correctly. Sometimes it might be that you need to look at multiple factors. Take the elder for instance. In the spring it has sprays of tiny white flowers that are edible, but it is also easily mistaken for other plants, particularly when it is a young specimen. However, some of these other plants such as hogweed or hemlock are extremely toxic. Giant hogweed grows to around 3.5 metres in height and so it's easy to see how this might be mistaken for an elder. If the sap comes into contact with the skin it can react to the sunlight and cause serious burns. Hemlock is extremely toxic and can cause death if ingested, causing heart attack like symptoms. However, misidentification can be avoided by looking at all of the pointers given above.

In my own foraging experience, when it comes to identifying plants, all of the above comes into play. Whilst it might sound like a lot of information to take in, the more you put it into practice, the easier it will become. You'll start to automatically look at the flowers, leaves, bark and so on to help you identify plants and trees. And once you recognise a plant, you'll start seeing it everywhere!

When and What To Forage

I go out all year round looking for goodies to harvest. Much of this is due to my location. Because I live in a valley, winters for me can be quite mild, in that snowfall is often light and some winters we don't get any snow at all. Early spring can also be sparse, with summer and autumn offering the highest yield, but there is always something that can be found in winter and spring.

Winter

• **Pine needles** can be eaten in a push during the winter months though the new growth towards spring are tastier.

- **Birch bark** can be used to make nourishing drinks.
- **Nuts and seeds** left over from the autumn months should also still be good.
- **Rosehips and haws** can still be found in winter left from the autumn. If they are still bright in color and reasonably firm then they will be good for eating, though perhaps not so great fresh. Process them and make fruit leathers and jellies.
- **Watercress** can be harvested during the winter months. Treat these as you would any other leafy greens.

Spring

- **Nettles**, both the stinging and dead varieties, are good for picking in the spring. The young leaves are tender and can be added to stews, soups, sauteed as they are or added to tea blends.
- **Dandelions** are often one of the first plants to come up in the spring. All parts are edible, from the flowers to the roots. The roots can be roasted to make a coffee substitute.
- **Chickweed** is another leafy edible that can be added to salads, soups, stews or sauteed.
- **Wild garlic** is an absolute delight, but do take care with this one. In the UK it is illegal to uproot plants in the wild and in some cases, the scarcity of wild garlic makes doing so seem somewhat irresponsible. However, the leaves are flavourful and good to use in cooking.
- **Plantain**, both the long leaf and broad leaf varieties, are edible but are best when the leaves are young and tender. The stalks are also edible.

- **Cleavers** (goosegrass) used to fascinate me as a kid, they were just so sticky! Cleavers are also edible and are best when still young.
- **Wild violets** are some of the first flowers to open in my part of the world. These too are edible and can be used in baking or on salads. I like to use them to create an infused honey that is just divine!

Summer

- **Fruits** such as wild strawberries can be found through mid to late summer, as can blackberries depending on your local area.
- There are so many **edible flowers** that are available in the summer that to list them all would require more space than I have now. Borage, cornflower, camomile, lavender, dog rose, common mallow and meadowsweet are just some of the very many and perhaps most common that you might find.
- **Clover** is good to eat by adding the flowers to salads. The stalks sauteed are also good to eat.
- Later on in the season, **elderberries** are abundant in my part of the world though do not eat too many of the raw berries. Instead make them into a health-promoting syrup.
- Soft fruits such as **gages** and **plums** will be ripe during august. Make the most of the fresh fruits by eating as they are. If they become overripe or bruised, then use them in puddings and jams.

Autumn

- **Sweet chestnuts** are one of my favorites and should you find any later on will be good for harvesting into the winter months.
- **Walnuts** are so good fresh from the tree and are so easily identified.
- **Hazelnuts,** both the common variety and the smaller but perhaps more tasty cobnuts are good. You can harvest them green or right through to early winter.
- **Rosehips and haws** are really good fresh.
- **Sloes** are the fruit from the blackthorn bush and whilst they are edible, they are extremely bitter, so much so that most use them to flavor alcohol, traditionally gin, though sloe vodka is equally as good.
- **Apples** and **pears** are in season now too. Eat them fresh from the tree and use the fallen or bruised fruit in cooking.
- **Crabapples** are also good for harvesting, and whilst these too can be eaten fresh, I prefer making jellies and jams with them.
- **Blackberries** will still be good well into autumn, even longer if the weather remains fair.
- **Burdock roots** can be harvested but pay attention to local bylaws.

There are so many edible plants that can be picked throughout the year that to list them all would require a book in itself. My advice is to find local interest books or identification books that are specific to where you live in the world and do some research into what can and cannot be eaten.

I also haven't included mushrooms and fungi in this section. I love foraging for mushrooms but it is a tricky business indeed. If this is an area you are interested in I've found the best way to go about it is to find a local person who knows what they are talking about. Using books is more difficult as quite often the differences between edible and poisonous varieties are difficult to spot.

Wild Cooking

So now you've gathered some wild grub, knowing how to prepare and cook it is the next challenge. Beginners often over think the cooking of foraged food but the key is to treat it in the same way you would foods you've purchased. Here I'll share with you some of my favorite recipes.

Dandelions: as already mentioned, all parts of this plant is edible. The flowers can be battered and deep fried or made into a tea but I must confess, the tea isn't a favorite of mine. Make a light batter and fry until they are a golden color, sprinkling with icing or confectioners sugar when they are fresh from the oil. For something a little more savory, add salt and pepper to your batter mix. I really enjoyed the stalks and the stems chopped and sauteed in butter with garlic (use your wild garlic leaves if you've been lucky enough to find some) and onion. You can also add them to dishes such as omelettes or salads. The leaves can also be lightly steamed and added to meals as you would other leafy greens.

Stinging nettles: be careful when handling these! The young leaves can be wilted or lightly steamed, or again, sauteed with onions and garlic. Nettle soup is tasty and healthy. Simply heat some oil over a medium heat and add onion and garlic, cooking until soft. Next add stock and any vegetables you like along with the nettle leaves and simmer until the vegetables are soft.

Nuts: of course these can be eaten straight from the tree as a tasty snack. With hazelnuts and sweet chestnuts though, I love to pan roast these with a little butter adding salt and pepper to taste. You can also roast them in their shells in a hot oven or even wrap them in foil and place in the embers of a low fire. I love to do this when camping, the perfect way to end an evening!

Flowers: many flowers can be eaten as they are fresh or are often added to baked goods as edible decorations. There are so many more things you can do with them though. They can be used to flavor wines as with elderflower wine (one of my favourites!). Simply place the elderflowers in a pan of water and fill with water so that they are just covered. Bring to the boil and allow to simmer for around half an hour. Strain the liquid into a clean pan and top up with fresh water until you have around 2 litres of water. Now add the sugar (roughly 1kg per litre and a half of liquid but this will depend on your own personal tastes and may require a little experimentation). When the sugar has dissolved, place the liquid into a demijohn or other sealable bottle and add a sachet of dried yeast (you can use wine making yeast though I use the ordinary stuff from my cupboard. I've tried both and can say I haven't noticed any difference in taste). Seal with an airlock, and voila. You should notice a foam to begin to form shortly after and the mixture should bubble away for weeks. When it has stopped bubbling, siphon into a clean bottle and leave to stand. Syphon at least twice more to remove any sediment and there you have it, homemade wine!

Soft drinks can also be made using flowers. Simply follow the same steps as when making wine but do not add yeast. You can add more sugar to make a cordial and this will also help preserve them. Elderflower cordial is a favorite of mine. Use fruit juice to make cordials as well. You can simply juice fruits such as apples, but for berries, place in a pan and cover with water and simmer, pressing the fruit with the back of a large spoon to get as much of the juice from the fruit as possible. Strain into a clean pan and add sugar, stirring until the sugar has dissolved.

I also like to infuse honey with flowers such as violets, roses, and lavender. Simply place in a jar and cover with honey. Leave for around a week and then strain into a clean jar.

Flavoured sugars are also a good way of using up any foraged flowers. Grind or shred the flowers, and add to normal granulated sugar, mixing thoroughly. Spread out on baking parchment and allow to dry before loosening the grains up and placing in a clean jar. You can use these sugars in baking, over cereals and in drinks.

Rosehips and hawthorn berries: use these super berries to make jams and jellies in the same way you would ordinary fruit jams and jellies. Remove the seed and use the flesh. They are particularly good when paired with apples, including crab apples. Prepare the fruit by deseeding, peeling and chopping. Use equal parts fruit and sugar and place in a pan with a little water. Heat slowly until the sugar has dissolved and allow to simmer for around half an hour or until the liquid has reduced by half. Make sure you stir often so as to avoid ruining your pans.

Barks and pine needles can also be eaten or used to make drinks, though when using pine needles make sure to choose a variety that isn't poisonous, and young shoots are best used. To make drinks simply boil in a pan of water and sweeten to taste. Barks can be eaten and should be boiled to soften before frying in oil or fat. Barks can also be ground to make flour.

Hunting

Now this part may be something you are simply not interested in for whatever reason and if you have any kind of moral dilemma about hunting animals for food or eating them then feel free to skip this section.

As a vegetarian myself, many marvel at my acceptance of hunting animals to eat. To understand my stance on hunting, we must consider the modern meat market, from farm to fork as the marketing phrase goes. The truth is, factory farming is on the rise and the animals raised and killed to fill the demand for cheap meat often live pain-filled lives.

The quaint and idyllic picture of farming we might hold is becoming something of a myth as consumers demand cheap meat and plenty of it. So what do we find instead? Pigs in cages with hardly enough room to turn over, barns full of poultry, so full they trample one another, and the birds themselves pumped so full of growth promoting hormones they cannot support their own weight.

I grew up and still live in a rural town in the middle of England, and my father was something of a poacher. A brace of rabbits was nothing new to the children my sisters and I once were, and though there was a sadness that these beautiful creatures had died, there was a necessity behind it, and the relationship to the land that underlies this way of getting food—that it fosters a respect for the land and the creatures that give sustenance—is some comfort. They lived a natural life, knowing not the misery of our modern meat animals and their death was not painful but rather quick and painless. To some, this doesn't matter. They will argue that an animal lost its life and that is that, but I would argue the difference is massive. Just watch any of the videos online about modern farming and slaughter practice. The difference is profound.

As I've already said, hunting may not be for you—many meat eaters do not have the stomach to catch and kill the meat they so readily buy wrapped in plastic from the supermarket shelf, which in turn makes hunting more sustainable and less about quality. I also think community and solidarity links come into play in this aspect too, that we can barter for those things we need with things we are able to make and produce ourselves.

In this section then, we will consider hunting methods and techniques of sourcing meat for the pot. Hunting for meat reinforces our link with nature and we come to realize we rely on it so much more than we ever did before. It is a symbiotic relationship, one that places us within nature as opposed to outside of it. The process of hunting for meat garners a respect for the animal, one that our modern day shopping and eating habits does not.

Shooting

I've already spoken about my upbringing and about my father who would often bring home a rabbit for the pot and one for the neighbor. For many, perhaps not nowadays but certainly when I was a girl, without these top up meals, they would have gone hungry.

Shooting is perhaps the best way of sourcing meat. The animal is killed quickly (a good huntsman will work on accuracy long before ever sighting an animal in their scope), with little in the way of pain and suffering. When it comes to shooting then it is important to choose the best tools for the job.

Here in the UK we have strict firearm laws. It is legal to own an air rifle below a certain power without a license and the most powerful of these will easily kill a rabbit or a pigeon. If the law is something you consider important and do not wish to break, then check out the local laws for where you live.

EMMA KATHRYN—*RECLAIMING OURSELVES*

Shotguns are well and good, but be sure to use the correct type of shot: you don't want to have to spend ages picking out shots from your meat. Shotguns are good for those who may struggle with the aim required for rifle shooting, and for larger prey such as deer. With that said though, a rifle is more than adequate to ensure at least some meat in your diet.

So you've got your gun and you've worked on perfecting your aim, what next?

It's important to know where to go hunting and what you'll be hunting for. It should go without saying: only kill what you intend to eat. I know some meat eaters find game to be, well, too gamey tasting and so then perhaps wild meat is not for you. Knowing what lives where is vital, as is making sure there is a healthy population to support mindful hunting. Part of sourcing wild food is understanding that to take too much is detrimental to the whole ecosystem, including us.

Where I live, rabbit is the game meat of choice and mostly because of the abundance. You will know when there is a healthy population of rabbit because you will see signs of them long before you spot one. Droppings are the biggest give away, and fresh droppings mean that they are active in that area. With rabbits, you'll often find grooves or ruts in the earth and when you're out and about, keep an eye on the edges of long grass and bushes. You'll see little runways through the scrub and undergrowth and these are made when rabbits pass to and from their burrows.

Once you've caught a rabbit for the pot, or any other animal for that matter, you will have to skin and gut them, not a pleasant idea I know, but a necessity if you want to eat wild meat. There are many good videos that will show you how to do this, but if all else fails, some butchers will offer this service.

Fishing

For many anglers in the UK, fishing is more of a hobby than done out of any real need for food and, again, there are strict laws about what fish and how many can be taken from water sources such as rivers and canals. As a girl, my dad would poach trout from local lakes but that is the extent to which my family would eat fish caught by him.

Learning to fish using a rod and reel is something that is being lost. An old colleague of mine showed genuine surprise when I told him that my sons both liked to fish. He had never been in his life and thus had never taken his own son, and this is quite a common scenario. How long before such knowledge is lost to us?

Basic rod set ups can be bought fairly cheaply and flea markets and car trunk sales are full of cheap secondhand rods. Skills such as setting up a rod with the correct weights and rig can be learned, either from videos of others who know, and anglers are a friendly bunch and will often help out beginners. There are different methods of fishing such as fly fishing (used mostly to catch trout) but simple line fishing is adequate and is also sustainable.

There are many good angling books out there that can teach you the basics better than I, and so check out second-hand shops or the internet for cheap books. I am a big fan of learning from books, and they can be kept for as long as you need them. Online videos are a great help as you can pause them until you get the hang of each part or action. There is much that will be learned from trial and error too, so don't be afraid to get out there and try things out. You'll soon get a feel for what works and what doesn't.

I'm not going to include any meat or fish recipes here, other than to say that for game meats, slow cooking is your friend and if the gamey taste is too strong for you, braising and slow cooking can make it more mild and palatable. Fish is fish and can be cooked however you like, oven baked or pan fried.

As I've already said, take what works for you and your own situation and discard the rest but whatever you do, beginning to make changes, no matter how small, is how it all starts.

Reclaiming Medicine

This section is in no way intended to replace medical attention for serious or life threatening illnesses and injuries, but we must recognize that Big Pharma is big business. Go to any cornershop, supermarket, or pharmacy and you will see a whole range of products that deal with all kinds of niggles and complaints, from headaches to coughs and colds right through to rubs for aching muscles and everything in-between.

Quite often these medicines aren't worth the money you pay for them. Take cough medicines for example. These do not cure the cough, for that is the body's own defense. A cough exists to rid yourself of what ails you. What such medicines do, however, is ease the symptoms of the cough. The syrupy texture coats the throat and eases any soreness or burning sensation. Honey does the same thing, as would a sugar syrup.

The truth is that we have forgotten, if we ever really knew in the first place, how to heal ourselves of common ailments. We've lost this knowledge and these techniques because of our ever-growing reliance on medicines as well as an expense for our convenience. When we are so busy working long hours, when we cannot afford to be ill, we have neither the time nor the effort required to make our own remedies. It's so much easier to nip to the pharmacy and buy what we need.

I must also say that I am not denigrating simple medicines—we've all popped a paracetamol or aspirin when we've had headaches and what not. Rather, I am suggesting that learning simple recipes and techniques can help alleviate some of our reliance on capitalist pharmaceutical manufacture.

In this section we will explore natural health remedies that include ingredients such as tree barks, plants, and flowers, as well as techniques that are beneficial in the treatment of common ailments.

I will also suggest that it will be beneficial to learn some basic first aid. Many charities offer short day-courses at reasonable prices, and they are well worth the money paid. First aid can and does save lives.

Techniques and Preparations

Before we go any further it is important to understand some of the basic techniques and preparations that can be used in the treatment of common ailments and complaints.

Teas: I am a big fan of medicinal teas. They are a great way of getting water, and the warming effect of the hot liquid aids wellbeing, especially when you are ill with fevers, coughs, and colds. Teas can be made loose leaf, or you can make tea bags easily enough, though using an infuser requires little effort.

Infusions: Similar to teas, infusions are waters or oils that have had herbs, spices and other plant matter added to them and left to infuse for a number of days or even weeks or over a low heat.

Decoctions: These are made by boiling the herbal or plant matter in water until the liquid has reduced by half. The plant matter is then removed. These can be drunk, or used in washes and waters.

Tinctures: Similar to infusions, these involve steeping plant matter in alcohol. Spirits with a high alcohol content such as vodka, rum, and brandy are used because some active ingredients are not water-soluble and therefore cannot be drawn from the plant into the liquid when using water.

Compresses: These can be used hot and cold. Clean cotton or bandages are dipped into a healing solution, perhaps a decoction or tincture, and used by placing over or wrapping around the affected area. These might be used to help treat burns, cuts, scratches, bites, etc..

Poultices: Similar to a compress, these are made with clean cotton or bandages. Wet plant matter such as macerated herbs are wrapped in the clean bandages and applied to the affected area.

Ointments and lotions: These are made by infusing herbs and other healing materials in oil. By adding other ingredients such as waxes or emulsifiers, you get ointments or lotions. These are applied directly to the skin and can treat a variety of minor ailments and conditions.

Basic Recipes for Minor Ailments

Cough Medicine

This simple medicine is not only for coughs but can be taken as a tonic and to help relieve the symptoms of colds and fevers.

You will need
- A clean jar
- Liquid ("runny") honey
- 2 inches (5cm) of ginger, roughly chopped
- A head of garlic, roughly chopped
- 1 onion, sliced

Simply layer the onion, garlic and ginger in the jar and pour over the honey until the ingredients are covered. Seal the jar and leave for at least a week on a warm windowsill, then drain the honey into a clean jar. Keep in the fridge and take either as a cold or cough remedy as often as needed or take a teaspoon every morning as a health tonic.

Elderberry Syrup

You can make this using sugar or honey, though of course honey will have more health benefits than sugar.

You will need:
- A clean jar
- Elderberries
- Honey or sugar
- A clean pan
- 2 -3 tablespoons (30-45 ml) of water

Place the elderberries in the pan with the water and add the same weight of honey or sugar. Heat gently, allowing the sugar to dissolve if you are using it. Continue to heat, drawing as much liquid from the berries as possible, then strain the mixture into a clean jar and refrigerate as needed. Take a spoonful when suffering from coughs, colds, fevers or the flu as often as needed or take a spoonful everyday as a health tonic.

Tincture of Thyme

Thyme, as many other herbs, has lots of medicinal and health improving qualities. Thyme is good for treating and easing the symptoms of respiratory issues as well as coughs and colds. To make a tincture, macerate (soften in water) the herbs and place in a clean jar. Fill the jar with a good quality spirit and allow to infuse for at least a week but up to a month. Strain into a clean bottle and take a spoonful as needed.

Warming Muscle Rub

This rub is great for those who exercise frequently and will help to ease those sore and aching muscles.

You will need:

• Hot chilli peppers (how many you include will depend on the heat of the peppers and the volumes made. Experiment until you have a heat level that you find warming but not uncomfortable).

• Oil of your choice. I use coconut oil because it is cheap and readily available but you can use whatever oil you choose.

• Beeswax (this is optional but will change the texture of the finished oil. I use a ratio of 3 parts oil to 1 part beeswax but again, experiment until you have a texture that suits you).

• A clean jar

Simply chop the peppers and place in a clean jar with the oils and beeswax. Heat the oil using the bain marie (double boiler) method, or place the jar in a pan of water and heat over a low heat. I use my slow cooker to infuse the oil for at least eight hours, stirring occasionally. Pour into a tin or jar and allow to cool. Use by massaging into the affected areas as needed.

Mugwort, Wormwood and Datura Ointment

This ointment, depending on the quantity of the ingredients used, can be psychoactive. The active datura is toxic if ingested, and together with wormwood and mugwort, should not be used by people with heart, liver, or kidney problems or by those who are pregnant, attempting to get pregnant or breastfeeding.

This ointment is good for helping with deep muscular and skeletal pain and can provide relief for pain from illness and conditions such as arthritis. The amounts I have suggested for this recipe are for a mild strength ointment. With regards to the mugwort and wormwood use equal quantities of each.

You will need:
- A clean jar
- 5g Dried mugwort
- 5g Dried wormwood
- 30 datura seeds
- Mortar and pestle
- Oil
- Beeswax (optional)

Use the mortar and pestle to grind the datura seeds. Place them in a clean jar with the dried plant matter along with the oil and beeswax and heat in a double boiler or place in a pan of water on a low heat or in a slow cooker for around 8 hours. You can also leave it to infuse on a warm windowsill for around 6 weeks before straining into a clean jar or tin and allowing it to cool. Use topically before bed to help alleviate deep muscular and skeletal pain.

Basic Cream Recipe

This is a basic recipe for a cream. The oils and tinctures added will determine the purpose of the cream. You will need:
- 10g beeswax
- 50ml of infused oil
- 20ml of tincture
- 20ml of infused water
- 5g of emulsifying wax
- 20 drops of essential oil

Heat the beeswax and the emulsifying wax in a bain marie along with the infused oil. In a separate pan gently heat the tincture and infused water but do not let boil. When both mixtures have cooled and pour into a clean bowl and whisk together until you have a creamy consistency. Add the essential oil and gently mix in.

These are all basic recipes you can use. Different herbs, flowers, spices and barks will have different healing properties and I've included a table to show the healing properties of common plants and herbs.

Plant, Tree, and Flower Healing Properties

Lavender: Antiseptic, anti-inflammatory, useful in the treatment of anxiety, insomnia, restlessness, depression, and acne.

Sage: Aids in digestion, diarrhea, loss of appetite, skin healing, can be used to help lower cholesterol, and to help respiratory problems. Antiviral, antibacterial.

St. John's Wort: Antiviral, can be used to help wounds heal, relieve menopause symptoms, and helps to treat depression and anxiety.

Chamomile: Aids sleep and relaxation, eases anxiety, high in antioxidants, reduces menstrual pain, reduces inflammation.

Willow: Willow can help in pain relief, particularly white willow. Teas, tinctures, powders etc can be made from the bark and young leaves.

Mint: Aids digestion, relieves stomach pain, can help lower breastfeeding pain, may help IBS. High in antioxidants.

Rosemary: High in antioxidants, anti-inflammatory, antimicrobial, insect repellant, aids circulation, and helps blood pressure.

Dock leaves: Useful in the treatment of burns, bites, cuts, scratches etc. The gel and sap from the leaves are the active ingredient, with the leaf itself being used as a bandage.

Tansy: Helps in the treatment of colds and fevers, gout, and kidney problems. Used in the treatment of threadworm and roundworm as well as lice. Promotes sweating and calms the nerves.

Of course, there are so many plants that are beneficial in healing, more than I have the space for here. There are many valuable books on herbal healing and the internet can also be a valuable source.

Reclaiming Land

Our relationship with the land is toxic. We find ourselves trapped within a capitalist system, one that views the land as a commodity. Land is treated as nothing more than a resource from which we can take and keep on taking, selling its plundered goods to the highest bidder with little or no care for the land or those who call it home. And it's a double-pronged attack on the land, as it becomes a dumping ground of waste, no matter the toxicity. It gets dumped along with anything else considered worthless or useless.

Within the capitalist system, many try and tread a little more lightly on the earth, trying to lessen the individual harm they might cause, but doing so is not easy. It can be downright difficult in fact, and at times outright dangerous. Attempting to protect the land against the onslaught of capitalism is a risky business indeed. At best, these people often find themselves the target of mockery and derision; at worst they have verbal, mental and physical abuse hurled at them from the champions of capitalism and the people who have been brainwashed by them.

We must also spare a thought for the poorest in society, who themselves may wish to lessen the burden they place on the land and environment but also have little or no choice but to buy the cheapest products and services. More often than not, such products and services are created by companies who are the biggest polluters, who cause the most harm to the land and those who reside there.

Already we can see the path ahead will be hard, fraught with danger and with the making of difficult decisions. Reclaiming the land will not be a comfortable process, but this section seeks to redress the balance. It aims to give the building blocks so that we can begin to realise and rebuild our connection to the land, uniting the spiritual and the mundane. As you've journeyed through the previous parts of this book, you will already have begun to see that we are not separate from the land or the earth. Maybe you've already begun to form a connection with the land where you live. At the very least, you will have begun to realise that our relationship with the land is a symbiotic one, and exploring this through the lens of food and medicine, you begin to see just how important that relationship is.

Before we go any further, it is important that we get an idea of just how we became so separated from the land in the first place and how that separation continues today.

What Once Was

When we think of the concept of common land, we usually tend to think about town or village greens: a communal outdoor—usually grassy—space used for activities such as games, festivals, and markets. Whilst these still exist in many towns and villages, they are usually governed by strict bylaws.

In the past, common land was so much more practical, and allowed those who were less fortunate or well-off to have access to the land. This access allowed the peasant classes to take what they needed: food, water, and resources such as fuel in the form of wood. This meant their survival and comfort was tied to the land.

To really understand how common land was used, we can look at the feudal system that existed from before 850 and is documented in the *Domesday Book* of 1086. Under the feudal system, all land basically belonged to the crown. This land was then placed in the care or stewardship of feudal lords. In exchange, the lords would provide resources and military service when required. The land, save for perhaps the most fertile or with the richest resources, was rented out or let to tenants for farming.

Whilst the feudal system did indeed work because of class division, with the crown at the apex and the peasants at the bottom with the lords in between, what we see is that the peasants, the common people, were very much connected to the land where they lived. The land that was considered less profitable was turned over to the common people for use, and here they could freely graze their animals, grow crops, and take resources such as water and wood. It would have been in their favor not to strip the land, but to care for it because their survival was linked to it. They recognised the symbiotic relationship and respected it.

Because of the nature of this common land, it would have been scattered across a wide area and because of this variability, decisions about the land were made communally. So we can see that despite class divisions, all people had access to the land and also that they worked closely with it and with one another.

Over time, with the onset of agricultural advancements and the industrial revolution, the rights pertaining to the common land were eroded. It's important to remember the industrial revolution also included farming, which meant the land that was once considered wasteland—that land given over to common usage—decreased. Increasing areas of land were fenced off as it passed into private ownership. At the same time, factories became the new workplaces of the poor, and so we can see how the loss of the commons forced the poor into wage labour.

With the access to the land taken from them, there was nowhere to raise or graze animals and no land from which to grow food or to take resources, no way to supplement their income or improve their living conditions. Industrialization continued to expand and people became increasingly disconnected from the land which had once sustained them.

Fast forward to today and we can see the extent of that separation from the land. The more we "progress," the more we become disconnected from it. And here we are, in a situation where children in towns and cities have no idea about where their food comes from, which in turn fosters ignorance and helps propel us into the realm of factory farming and the destruction of our wild places. It seems that we've forgotten that no matter how technologically advanced we become, we still rely on the land for our very survival. But even without considering food and survival, today when so many of us spend the majority of our day working long hours, living in ever increasing urbanised areas, the availability of green space, never mind wild space, adds to the problem of disassociation.

If we then consider how much we have come to depend on technology and not just for work and communication but also for relaxation, that means that the time we spend outside is decreasing. When we come home from work or have a day off we are often too mentally and physically exhausted to do little more than sit in front of screens. And it doesn't matter that these activities are not relaxing (and can be quite the opposite): we've become accustomed to this lifestyle. The separation between us and the land, it would seem, is all but complete.

What Connection Means

The previous sections of this book, despite not having connection to the land as a focus inevitably foster the beginnings of relationship, because food and medicine begin with the land. It is the connection to land and to nature that underpins everything, whether we realise it or not. But what does this connection look like in our everyday lives?

For each of us, this connection and relationship with the land will look a little different. After all, we are all individuals with unique thoughts and feelings, living in different parts of the world in a variety of situations and contexts. Ultimately though, as different as we all are, there are some basic commonalities. Perhaps the first and most obvious is not causing deliberate harm out of laziness. It also means becoming stewards of the land where we live, that we fight the injustices against the land as best we can, in whatever way we can. It is the understanding and realization that we are not separate from the land or from each other, no matter what capitalism would have us believe, that we are as much a part of nature as the birds, beasts, trees and plants. We are not the Overman. We have not triumphed over nature, because to do so would bring our own destruction.

It all sounds a bit dire, doesn't it? But there is hope. As I write this part of the book, I find myself in lock down amid the coronavirus pandemic. Whilst the fear surrounding this virus is very real, the enforced lockdown has shown that many people are beginning to realise just how important the land and nature is to their physical and mental wellbeing, that connection to and relationship with the land is everything. It's also demonstrated how quickly the land will self heal when given time to do so. And so let us now turn our attention to the many practical ways we can begin on the path towards reconnection deepening our relationship with the land.

Putting Your Money Where Your Mouth Is

Reducing our impact on the environment, "saving the planet," is not an easy task considering it goes against the grain of everything we've been conditioned to believe. That's why the rich talk about carbon offsetting every time they hop aboard their private jets as though that makes everything okay. Protecting the environment, or at least how it's pushed by the powers that be, has become just another facet of big business, of capitalism. It's become just another way to extort money from people and usually those people who pay the most are the poorest in society.

Let us consider the motor industry and the taxes that surround it in the U.K. as a prime example. There's no denying just how harmful the motor industry and car usage is in terms of not only the air pollution caused by vehicles but also the impact of the oil and petroleum industries. Now some years ago, the government of the time put in place tax measures that favoured or fostered a move towards diesel vehicles instead of petrol, believing (or so we're told) that this was the lesser of two evils. This dash for diesel saw a massive increase of diesel vehicles on U.K. roads. Fast forward to today, where diesel is heavily taxed both at the pump and in terms of the emissions or road tax. Not only that, the government wants to ban diesel cars as well as those vehicles that are over a certain age, due to the levels of pollution they emit, and as per usual, it will be the poorest who have to pay the price.

Government and business schemes then, to many people, seem just another way of parting people from their money. The push for electric cars is just another example of a superficial concern for the environment. All too often, many people do not think about how that electricity is generated, either from massive coal burning or nuclear power stations, nor from where the lithium for the batteries will come and who will have to mine for it. The environmental costs of these mines is massive, and that's without counting the human cost to the poorest people who will have little choice but to work in such places. When we dig a little below the surface, we see that these schemes aren't as green as we might wish they are.

But with that said, it's easy to see why people want to believe. When we feel so helpless and maybe even hopeless, we want to cling to any glimmer of hope. We want to believe we can buy our way out of the environmental problems we face. It eases our guilt, if only just a little. We've grown used to token gestures, because all too often that's the only power we feel we have and the truth often comes as an inconvenience. More than that though, the truth has a nasty habit of making our efforts seem futile and makes us question what the point actually is. This delusion or ignorance when faced with the truth is a defense mechanism.

So what then? If everything is as bleak as it would appear, if our efforts to save the environment are little more than cash cows, does this then mean that all of our efforts are pointless? I don't believe so. Individual efforts can make a difference even if that difference is in our own lifestyles, even if it means we ourselves tread a little more lightly on the earth. This will help foster a relationship with the land.

I often say to people that the only real choices we have in this world are what to think and where we spend our money. These last bastions of freedom are always under attack, but we can make the choice to buy our necessities with a green mind, buying, where finances allow, from those individual, local businesses and from those whose business plan includes caring for the environment. These small changes to our shopping habits are perhaps the easiest to implement.

The problem with many eco-products is that not only are they often more expensive than their regular counterparts, but many large corporations have jumped on the band-wagon to ensure they don't lose out on their share of the profits. Already we can see how the poorest are priced out, forced to rely on the most polluting products. And for any readers that do indeed fall into that category, do what you need to do to survive without guilt, for the guilt belongs firmly at the feet of big business. I've been in the position of having to choose between my morals and beliefs and feed-ing my family many, many times before, and it is a horrible situation to find yourself in. Really it's no choice at all and you will find no blame here.

But being in that position does give you an insight into what items you really need, and which are little more than a frivolous luxury. When you come out of the other side, those lessons in frugality serve you well. After all, one of the biggest problems we have today is that of wastage, and you'll already be well-versed in getting the most from those items and products you have available to you.

Choosing to buy from independent producers, cottage industries, and markets is a good option. You often find that the goods are of better quality and these small busi-nesses can't afford waste in the way that corporations and chain stores can. Instead of adding to the coffers of big business, you'll be putting money in the pockets of people within your local community.

Cutting down on plastic is something else we can do that requires very little effort. Taking cloth bags when we go shopping, opting for those products with less packaging, means that at the very least, there's less plastic in your own life. I hate plastic with a passion and so reducing it is only ever a good thing. It can seem like such a small thing but imagine if everyone did it. Imagine the impact it would have. But we can't always concern ourselves with the practices of other people, sometimes we have to concentrate on getting ourselves right first so that our relationship with the land is not based on hypocrisy.

Using whatever influence we have and encouraging others to consider the land, environment, and nature, showing them what can be achieved is a great way of affecting change, even if it is a drip effect. It's also a great way of building connection with others, fostering community links and building those mutual aid and solidarity networks. We can also think about direct action including protesting. The internet, in particular social media means we can share what we have learned and our own endeavors far and wide. Using our talents—whether that's writing, art, or public speaking—is a great way of spreading the message, and the arts in particular have a massive impact on both the heart and mind.

Usually though, it is often the people nearest to us, such as family members and friends, who have the biggest influence on us. We are more inclined to listen to them than a stranger. Even having discussion and debate with people of opposing beliefs is a good way of challenging the mentality, the status quo and the fact that these discussions are happening is important. The change in mindset and habits must begin somewhere.

Getting Out Where You Live

It doesn't matter where in the world you live, be it the countryside or more urban areas like towns and cities. You can build a relationship and reclaim your connection to the land right there. Making an effort to get out daily, even if it's for a short walk or sitting somewhere you feel relaxed and safe is perhaps the easiest way of building a relationship with the land. Getting out into your local community also gives you first hand insight into any environmental issues that might otherwise have been missed. For example, I live on a council estate in the middle of England and as I write this, the council are looking to demolish many homes in order to build more. Many of the residents, in fact all of them I've spoken to, are up for this, taken in by the allure of a new house. I am actively against the proposals.

The difference between myself and my neighbours, or at least as far as I can see, is my connection to the land where I live. Where others see just a council estate, I see trees, plants, and animals. I see ecosystems that will be lost because there will be less green spaces after the redevelopment and fewer wild places. And I have gone down all of the usual routes of protesting, the socially-accepted routes to no avail. Still, I try because what else is there to do? I guess the point I'm trying to make is that it is my intimate knowledge of the area, my connection to it that urges me to argue for it. It is my relationship to this land that makes me want to fight for it, whether the odds are stacked against me or not. It is this very connection to the land that allows me to see it with different eyes to that of my neighbours, that lets me see it for what it is: alive and thriving. And I wouldn't have such a connection if not for being outside, walking, immersing myself in it.

By spending time outside in your local areas you also begin to form community links which can be very important. When the community comes together, when single voices of dissent and protest merge together, it can be very powerful indeed. My small town has a modest library in the centre. The library itself sits in beautiful gardens fronted by a car park. A few years back, the council wanted to chop down beautiful mature trees in order to create six more car parking spaces. But to my joy, local citizens formed an action group and the trees remain. A small victory perhaps in the grand scheme of the destruction of nature, but a victory nonetheless.

It's important to remember that these small victories are vital, not only because of the cumulative effect of many of them, but also because these victories makes people realise that they do have the power to affect the change they want to see in the world.

Appreciating and protecting the green and wild places we have left is not only important in terms of limiting environmental damage but it's action that can help deepen your relationship to the land.

Spiritual Reclamation

So far we have looked at our physical impact upon the environment and land, as well some ways we might reduce that impact as a way of deepening our connection to it. Now let us turn our minds towards our spiritual connection to the land, and how we might reclaim that connection. Every part of this book so far, in some small way, has started us on the path to reclaiming the land, not only physically but spiritually as well.

As an animist I see the whole world as being imbued with spirit, from the city streets to the wild woods and everything in-between. It is this spiritual connection to the land many have lost, whether because of the time spent in wage labour and the toll it takes on us or the subsequent reliance on convenience food and medicine. Regaining this spiritual connection and reclaiming the land involves work, but most of that work is enjoyable and fulfilling. It involves taking time from our daily routines to really see the land as a living, sentient body. More often than not the hardest part is the very beginning, trying to break the regular routines and habits that govern our everyday lives. It does get easier though. The more we get our minds around the momentous task, the easier it becomes. The more you get used to being in nature, the more time you will want to spend within it, which in turn leads to a deeper connection.

The sacredness of the land is something we have lost sight of as a species. The capitalist system sees nothing as sacred, not the land, nor nature, nor those who live within it —including us. Within capitalist societies, we are nothing more than resources to be exploited for the benefit of the few. Also, making us feel that the land and everything else is anything but sacred makes it easier to separate us from it. If we thought the land was indeed sacred, then we would do more to protect it.

I do think the tide is turning, especially now we have found ourselves within a recent pandemic. People are beginning to realize the positive effect nature has on all aspects of our wellbeing, and in doing so they are beginning to sense the sacredness of nature and the land. It is a slow process, because of the system of living they have grown accustomed to, but for those of you who have found your way here, I suspect it is something you've known for a while. The spiritual connection to the land once you have passed this point becomes easier and the work I've mentioned really isn't that difficult beside making the time to fit it in somewhere. This work can take the form of sitting beneath a tree and paying attention to the minute details, it might be letting your feet dangle in a cool stream on a warm summer's day, listening to the chatter of the flowing water. It might be meditating on the grass and feeling the earth beneath you. All of these things and more besides can be considered as spiritual work. Not so hard after all, eh? And besides, spirit recognises spirit, which makes it all the more easier once we have broken the chains of routine.

These simple activities work on many levels. In the first instance, it gives people space and time to just be. This sounds so very simple doesn't it? But try telling that to someone who has to work 40 plus hours a week, especially when that work is physically demanding. Try telling this to someone who is struggling to survive, who has constant money worries and stress. Try telling it to someone who is overwhelmed with the world. More often than not, folks endure all of those issues at the same time and so the idea of just going somewhere and sitting can seem frivolous, a waste of time and effort. It can feel, at first, as though it takes away vital time and resources from tackling the issues at hand but the opposite is true. Giving yourself the space and time to just be and to enjoy being outside gives us a much needed break from the stress of the struggle that is trying to survive. It is good for our mental, physical and spiritual health. Before long, you'll come to appreciate the importance of these times and recognise the benefits they provide.

Once you have made the effort, as already mentioned, it gets easier, becomes part of your routine. If you keep it up for any length of time, particularly if you visit the same place, you'll begin to become familiar with the nuances of it. You'll slowly begin to notice the fauna that lives there, lose yourself in the activities of birds and insects. It's amazing really, this transformation, this finding of magic in the mundane and this is the beginning of forming a connection with that place, with the land. You'll become aware of seasonal changes, of the natural cycles and rhythms of that place and as you become more familiar with it, you'll start to see it for what it really is, a living sentiant being. You'll see how the parts come together to create the whole, and in doing so you'll understand that we are a part of this too. This is when we become close to the spirit of the land. Often times, when we think of spirituality or spirit work, we see or understand the term 'spirit' to mean something other, but here we realise that spirit work is centred in our real, lived experiences.

Reclaiming the Body

The war on our bodies is waged on all fronts, and bodies have become a battleground for the norms of modern society.

The effects of this war can be seen most clearly on our physical bodies, especially on our looks. At the extreme ends of the spectrum we have eating disorders such as anorexia or morbid obesity, both the physical manifestation of psychological warfare. We are constantly fed ideas concerning the perfect height, weight, shape, colour or shade of body and skin, led to believe that if we only look a certain way then we'll get our happy ever afters.

These ideas are sold to us in a myriad of forms. We see them in film, in television, in advertising, and in books where the protagonist is miserable because they don't fit the physical norms of whatever society they belong to. It doesn't matter that they have so much to offer, be that sharp wit, academic achievement, boundless talent: their lives are depicted as not worth living. Until, that is, they undergo some massive makeover where they completely change their appearance and suddenly they've got the perfect life, their happy ending.

Of course this attack on the body goes much deeper than physical looks, for we are more than our appearance. Mind, body, and soul are inextricably linked, and an attack on one is an attack on all. That attack begins with the making of the 'slave body.'

To be totally honest, I can't remember when or where I came upon this idea, only that I read it in a book and remember the profound effect it had on me straight away. The book claimed the slave body was the sitting body. At first I didn't understand what it was saying, but I know it made me feel like I had to think about it more. Like most things that make us change our mind, the first reaction was an emotional one. At the time, I worked in a physical job that involved standing for nine hours a day, humping heavy boxes up and down two flights of stairs. Of course I was going to come home after work and sit down—how rude of the author to suggest this made my body a 'slave body!'

But then I realised what the author was getting at. The slave body is the person who is but a cog of the capitalist system, who, after working hard all day comes home and sits down in front of a screen. They eat convenience food and go to bed, ready to do it all again the next day, and the day after, and so on and so forth. And for many who work physically demanding, underpaid jobs with little or no job satisfaction, this is how the attack on the body really begins in earnest.

We are encouraged to look after ourselves not because of our own health, but so that we remain in good working order, so that we don't take too many sick days. We no longer work to live but rather live to work.

But just like nature, our bodies are sacred. So we shall explore ways of reclaiming the body, not for anyone else's benefit, but for ourselves.

Body Image & Self Worth

Anyone who is different will no doubt have grown up with body image issues and even perhaps issues relating to self worth. It doesn't matter whether the difference was physical or economic, both are equally visible. In many cases the differences are both physical and economic, as one often leads to the other.

That's how it was for me. As a mixed race girl, growing up on a poor council estate in the middle of England, my differences were so very obvious. My family were poor and so new clothes were almost unheard of, and by the time hand-me-downs got to me, they'd already been worn by my two older sisters. I remember being about six or seven and thinking of my peers at school as Disney Girls. I think I meant the term to encompass all they represented and all of the things I so very clearly wasn't. They came to school in pretty dresses, with ribbons in their straight, shiny hair and nice new shoes. Their mothers would pick them up from the school gates, their clothes of the latest trend, their hair permed to perfection.

I on the other hand was the only brown girl in the whole school, save for my younger sister who would have been in the adjoining nursery. My hair was a tangle of curls, my clothes hand-me-downs. Even then, I knew there were clear differences in the way I looked compared to my peers and these only became more pronounced as I hit my teenage years. Then, like so many others, I became conscious of my changing body and as I became more aware of the societal norms and expectations surrounding physical appearance, I knew I didn't fit into them.

So many of us experience this and so many of us would have changed ourselves to fit in if only we could, so heavy do our differences weigh on us. Of course now, as an adult, I wouldn't change who I am, but when we are young and being different often means we are a target, it's hard to stay true to oneself. Selling out can be a form of self preservation, of self defense. Being on the outside opens us up to mockery, degradation and worse. And when we become adults, we carry the scars of our childhoods with us as emotional baggage in the form of poor self-esteem and negative body image.

Our work through this section will go some way to heal those scars, to show us that self worth is not defined by how we look, and that the body image we have been sold as perfect our whole lives is deeply flawed.

Exercise and Fitness

Related to the issue of self worth, body image and the concept of the slave body is exercise. We all know the importance of exercise on health and well being, mental as well as physical, and yet so many of us do not have an exercise regime and many of us baulk at the idea.

In part this is because we give so much of ourselves in our work lives. I know how it feels after a hard day's work, to want nothing more than to sit down and watch mindless TV that requires no thought, to rest until it all begins again the next day, but this is a fallacy and is part and parcel of the slave body. I also know from experience that exercise gives us more energy and makes us feel better in ourselves. We can all exercise, whatever our current health or fitness levels and exercise can be differentiated for those with mobility issues.

You do not have to join a gym or buy any equipment to begin exercising, indeed exercise is one of those activities that is accessible to all regardless of economic status. I will say though that if you have considered joining a gym but have been put off by your preconceptions, then be brave and bite the bullet: you might just find you are pleasantly surprised. In my own experiences of going to the gym, the people who go there despite how they might look are genuinely helpful and encouraging. They too started somewhere. But a gym setting is not for everyone nor is it always in everyone's budget.

Finding an exercise programme will need you to consider your current health and fitness levels and it's important to be honest with yourself. Starting an exercise regime too fast, doing more than your body can cope with too soon is not only physically dangerous (you can make yourself more vulnerable to injury) but it can also hold you back mentally, making you feel like a failure or that exercise just isn't for you, you just can't do it and so you give up even trying. Setting yourself ridiculously hard targets to achieve is another way of setting yourself up for failure. Be kind to yourself and build your fitness up slowly. It doesn't take as long as you might think. Here then let us consider a range of different exercises and regimes.

Walking

Walking is perhaps the most underrated of exercises. So many people beginning their exercise journeys are so eager to see results they often overlook the simpler forms of exercise because they think they are not rigorous enough. However, walking is a fantastic way to start. It's good for posture, works the core muscles, calves, glutes, hamstrings, and quads. If you build it up so you are covering a good distance at a moderate speed it's also a good calorie burner and certainly aids weight loss. It's a low impact exercise that doesn't stress the joints in the same way as running or weight training. It's also a brilliant way of getting outside more and we've already seen how that corresponds to connecting to the land and foraging.

Jogging

The next step up from walking and a natural progression if you decide it's something you might want to try. A higher impact exercise than walking, jogging will improve aerobic fitness and will burn more calories than walking as it makes the body work harder. Because it's higher impact, a thorough warm up and cool down before and after will help reduce the likelihood of injury.

Running

People often assume that running and jogging are the same. While it's true they are very similar, running is about moving faster, about pushing yourself. For example, you can jog a two mile course going at the same steady pace all the way around; however when running the same course, you'll be pushing your endurance so that each time you are completing the course faster than the last. Running is high impact and warming up properly is a must, along with dynamic stretching. Running is hard work, there's no doubt about it but again, it's a natural progression from jogging. As hard as it might be, the benefits from running are many, including an increase in aerobic and anaerobic fitness. It works the core muscles, especially the obliques and it is a fantastic calorie burner.

Sprints

There's nothing quite like sprints to push yourself to your limits. I used to do these when preparing for a fight, as they replicate the fight experience more than any other exercise. Sprints involve running for a short set distance then sprinting as fast as you can for the same distance. The idea is you sprint, then run, then sprint, then run, and so on for a set number of reps or for a timed round.

When I do these I use the football pitch markings on the local field. I start at one end then run to the halfway line, then sprint to the end before turning around and repeating. I'd usually set a time limit so if the fight I was training for had 2 minute rounds, I'd do 3 minute rounds of sprints for 5 sets, building it up each week. A good way to incorporate these into your running is when you are almost home, to use lamp posts as markers for your sprints. Not everyone will want to do these, but they are a really good fat burner as well as a fantastic way of increasing anaerobic fitness.

Circuit Training

I love a good circuit! Circuit training is great for people who get easily bored with doing just one form of exercise such as jogging or running, and a well thought out circuit will work your whole body. You can adapt and differentiate a circuit to suit your capabilities and you don't need any expensive or specialized equipment.

For those unfamiliar, a circuit involves doing a range of exercises for a set amount of time before moving on to the next. A simple circuit might involve doing 2 minutes of squats, 2 minutes of push ups, 2 minutes of sit ups and so on with a short rest period between each one. You can increase the intensity so that you might do 30 seconds of each exercise going flat out, really pushing yourself with 30 seconds rest between each exercise. You can adapt them however you want: circuit training is extremely adaptable.

Body Weight Training

Using your own body weight to increase muscle strength and stamina as well as toning and building lean muscle is great because you don't need any extra equipment, just your own body. Examples of body weight exercises include push ups, squats, lunges, tricep dips, mountain climbers, burpees and pull ups. You can incorporate them into circuit training or add them on to the end of a walk, jog or run to add a little something extra.

Creating a Workout Regime

To get started on the journey of strengthening your body, all that is required is a little planning. It's often quite tempting to skip this step, but I would wholeheartedly advise that you don't. Having a plan, whether it's just a piece of paper you can pin somewhere you'll see it or a fancy electronic spreadsheet doesn't matter, they both serve the same purpose.

A set plan motivates you. It gives you a week by week workout guideline so you don't need to think of what to do when. This is perhaps one of the biggest reasons people stop exercising. They lose sight of how to achieve their end result. A clear plan that includes progression allows you to look back and see how far you've come. It also means you don't really have to think about your workout as you already know what you'll be doing and on what days. This way, working out becomes a normal part of your daily routine.

Here I will give two examples of a workout plan. The first one involves walking, jogging or running as part of your regime. The second is an example circuit and the third combines the two.

Programme 1

This workout is aimed at beginners who haven't exercised for a very long time and perhaps don't have the confidence to approach a more strenuous workout programme straight away. You will notice how it builds up each week in small ways. It is important not to make it too hard too soon but to instead create a smooth progression.

Week 1

Monday: 2 minutes of dynamic stretching. 1 mile brisk walk. Cool down stretches.
Tuesday: Rest Day

Wednesday: 2 minutes of dynamic stretching. 1 mile brisk walk. Cool down

Thursday: Rest Day

Friday: 2 minutes of dynamic stretching. 1 mile brisk walk. Cool down

Saturday & Sunday: Rest Day

Week 2

Monday: 2 minutes dynamic stretches. 2 mile walk alternating speeds. 2 minute cool down.

Tuesday: Rest Day

Wednesday: 2 minutes dynamic stretches. 2 mile walk alternating speeds. 2 minute cool down.

Thursday: Rest Day

Friday: 2 minutes dynamic stretches. 2 mile walk alternating speeds. 2 minute cool down.

Saturday & Sunday: Rest Day

Week 3

Monday: 2 minutes dynamic stretching. 2 mile walk but for the last half mile alternate 2 minutes of walking with 30 seconds jogging.

Tuesday: Rest day

Wednesday: 2 minutes dynamic stretching. 2 mile walk but for the last half mile alternate 2 minutes of walking with 30 seconds jogging.

Thursday: Rest day

Friday: 2 minutes dynamic stretching. 2 mile walk but for the last half mile alternate 2 minutes of walking with 30 seconds jogging.

Saturday & Sunday: Rest Day

Programme 2

This is a circuit based programme that includes 10 different exercises. As with the programme above it includes variations and progressions and can be done by beginners who are a little more confident in their ability. Each circuit utilises the same exercises however the difference is in the timing of each exercise and rest period.

Each circuit contains the same exercises. It's so important to make sure you have a rest day following a workout day as it gives your body important recovery time.

Circuit 1:

These are 2 minute rounds with 1 minute exercise between each round. You can do as many reps or take it more slowly during the round. This is about pacing yourself.

Start with a 2 minute warm up including dynamic stretches and finish with a cool down and a thorough stretch.

1. Running on the spot (bring your knees up as high as possible)
2. Starjumps
3. Pushups
4. Situps

5. Lunges
6. Tricep dips
7. Squats
8. Mountain climbers
9. Shadow boxing
10. Plank

Circuit 2:

This time you do 10 of each exercise before moving on to the next exercise with no rest. After completing all of the exercises, take a 2 minute rest. Complete 3 - 5 sets.

Circuit 3:

Still using the same exercises, this time do 1 exercise per round. The rounds are 1 minute each, but you work for 30 seconds then rest for 30 seconds. During the exercise period of each round, you push yourself as hard and fast as you can, after all, it's only 30 seconds. After completing all of the rounds, have a 2 minute rest and then repeat.

There's absolutely nothing stopping you from mixing it up and changing any exercises you really cannot do. You might even choose a fitness programme that incorporates elements from both, so you might walk or jog twice a week and do circuit training once a week. These are just some examples of how you can incorporate an exercise programme into your life. Keep in mind that they don't take up that much time either. A brisk 2 mile walk might only take you half an hour, and the circuits I've suggested should take no longer.

Self Defence

Self defence is an important part in the reclamation of our bodies. To a certain extent, we've already begun the process by improving and increasing our general fitness. As someone who has fought in the boxing and kickboxing ring, I can tell you now that being physically fit is of the utmost importance when it comes to fighting. But in general everyday terms, being physically fit or improving our fitness is itself a self defence, since it makes us stronger and more able to fight back against attackers and oppressors. It's also defence against negative thoughts and feelings, as well as a defence against the concept of the slave body.

Here though we are going to talk about actual self defence, that is, the art of fighting back. I know that not everyone is interested or even physically able to defend themselves against physical attack and this is another intersection where solidarity and community mutual aid networks can play a massive role. That said, let us consider what fighting back, what self defence offers us. For myself, as a woman of colour who grew up and still lives on a 'rough' council estate, being able to defend myself has meant I've been able to traverse this world with the confidence that stems from being able to do that. It's meant I haven't had to be afraid. It's meant that I can do the things I want to do without being overly worried. As the rapper KRS says, 'to stay on course means to role with force.' In other words, being able to defend yourself, rolling with force, means being able to achieve what it is you want because others will know you ain't playing!

Martial arts are a fantastic way of building fitness while at the same time learning to defend yourself. I am a firm believer that there is a martial art for everyone, it's just a case of finding something you enjoy. When it comes to choosing a combat method, you might find yourself limited by what's on offer where you live but I'm a silver lining kind of woman and so suspect there will be something you enjoy or that suits you. Most clubs offer a free trial session, and you should take full advantage of this as it allows you to get a feel for the club and the sport before committing or spending any money.

There are pros and cons to all martial arts so don't get too hung up on which martial art is best for self defence. Purists of any sport will tell you theirs is the best and martial arts is no different, but each of them offer techniques that are practical in a real world situation. As someone who has practised boxing, kickboxing, muay thai and grappling, I can tell you that they all have given me something that I could use to defend myself.

More than anything else though, something that can be gained from any combat sport is the fighting mentality. Learning to fight is more than just going along to a boxercise class. In the gym, there are many types of people who all come to train for their own reasons. Some of them will be there purely for fitness, whilst others enjoy the sport in a non-combative way—they just enjoy coming down and hitting the pads and bag. Then there are the fighters. The difference between the fighters and the others is that of mentality, of mind set. The truth is to be successful in any kind of fighting—whether in the ring or in real life situations —you need to train hard. You need to push yourself past physical pain and self doubt. You must train so that the techniques you've learned come naturally, in the heat of the moment, when you are stressed and under pressure.

Do not let all of that put you off though, it is a good feeling, honest! The hard training, the sheer guts and hard work, the breaking down and building back up of the self and the ego not only provides physical fitness and the ability to defend oneself, but also develops a healthy body image. That image comes from knowing the journey your body and mind have been on, from understanding the struggles you have overcome, and knowing you can rely on your body to be strong and do what you need it to do.

Training in terms of becoming proficient at fighting is indeed hard work, but I can't stress enough how enjoyable it is. It sounds odd I know, but there is a real sense of fulfillment and achievement that comes from putting yourself through your paces. When you find the martial art that suits you, that you enjoy, it makes all of the hard work worth it.

So how does martial arts help when it comes to self defence? Besides teaching you how to hit, kick, lock, and take down an opponent, you might come across the idea that martial arts do not translate well into real life situations.

I've heard it many times before and usually from people who have never really trained seriously with self defence and fighting in mind. They'll say that in the street you aren't wearing your training clothes, and when it comes to women they'll probably be wearing high heels and tight clothing. The truth is that sometimes you might find yourself wearing clothes that aren't the best suited to combat or self defence, but more often than not, in those real life scenarios, you will only need a couple of well placed shots that are enough to stun your attacker and allow you to get away safely or make them have second thoughts.

Another argument is that people freeze in the moment. But that's the purpose of all of your hard work in the gym. It's this hard work that makes fighters different. It's also what sparring is for. Sparring is simultaneously my favourite thing to do in the gym and the thing I hate the most! It's a weird headspace to be in, willingly getting in the ring, knowing that you are going to get punched and kicked and that you are going to punch and kick. I always found sparring harder than actual fights with unknown opponents, because you know the strengths of your teammates and you have to fight against that knowledge. Oftentimes my teammates were bigger, stronger and better than myself and it is a daunting experience but it's also exhilarating and as my coach often says, iron sharpens iron.

You improve by learning from your sparring partners and sometimes you don't always see that improvement until later when you get your arm raised at the end of a fight or you've successfully defended yourself against a would-be attacker. The point I'm making is that we train hard to become proficient in all scenarios, whether that's the gym, ring or street. It's the overcoming of our own fears and the reactions that occur in our own bodies such as the adrenaline spike, that allow us to apply our knowledge in the real world and to be successful when doing it.

Reclaiming Paganism and Witchcraft

Many people find their way to paganism and witchcraft as adults, sometimes after becoming disillusioned with other, more mainstream religions and spiritualities and because they've finally found a name for something they've felt their whole lives. When they find it, it's like a sparkling treasure trove where there are no rules or boundaries, they are free to practise and believe whatever they so wish (or so it can seem at first). It is liberating to finally be able to recognise and name something you've felt for years.

Unfortunately however, as with so many spiritualities and belief systems, capitalism has sunk it's claws into this sphere of worship and practise. Plastic trinkets, resin statues, crystals torn from the earth, synthetic incense and perfumes or those made from endangered plant species, books that share the same misinformation over and over, the list of capitalism's crimes against paganism and witchcraft goes on and on.

Or you join social media groups in the hope of finding like-minded people with whom you can have meaningful discussion and debate only to realise that most of these groups aren't worth your time or effort (of course, some groups are better than others, but the good are outweighed by the bad, massively so). All too often conversations abound about which crystal heals a specific social/economic/ emotional/physical problem, someone reminding you about the threefold law or karma, and people who give their opinion as fact without considering issues with an open mind.

It's easy to become disillusioned, easy to think this is all there is, that there is no deeper meaning or connection. Most of us have felt this way in the past, so much so that we think that maybe we aren't that which we thought we were, that the terms 'pagan' and 'witch' don't apply to us. Sometimes it feels like the terms have become synonymous with live action role playing or cosplay. Of course there is nothing wrong with these but they have nothing to do with spirituality.

Many of us feel like we have nothing in common with the wider mainstream pagan or witch communities. A close friend of mine lately declared that he's hardly pagan anymore, and not because his beliefs have changed but because he doesn't really have much in common with mainstream paganism. And I have to agree with him. Any pagan event is full of people wearing crushed velvet, nylon fairy wings and plastic unicorn horns and when in that situation, it's glaringly obvious just how much you don't have in common with the white washed, polite paganism that is prevalent today.

All of these issues means that those practitioners who truly believe in the spiritual and magickal aspects of paganism and witchcraft often feel like they do not belong and so are driven away from it.

I don't really like labels. They are just so limiting, and once you attempt to label something it ceases to be that which it was before, instead becoming narrower and smaller. However, for the sake of communication, labels do serve a purpose even though their limiting effect makes it so that much of the meaning and nuance is lost.

With that said, let me tell you what I mean when I talk about paganism and witchcraft. When it comes to paganism then, I mean all religions and spiritualities that fall outside of the monotheistic religions. I also mean a spiritual system that sees nature and the land as being alive and imbued with spirit, where there is a deep reverence for nature and a recognition of our place within it. When I talk about witchcraft, I mean the practise of magick, both the application and theory. I mean working with the energies and spirits of the universe to affect change. I also include *malefica* in my meaning.

I consider myself to fall into both of these categories when using these brief understandings of them. I call myself witch because I practise witchcraft. I consider myself animist because I see the world as being imbued with spirit and alive. I call myself pagan because of the reverence I feel for nature, because of my animist beliefs. To be honest though, when I am just me at home, in my everyday life, I don't really think about what I am. I just am, and I suspect many people feel that way about themselves. I don't think anyone really thinks of themselves in terms of labels, except when trying to convey meaning to others.

The Problems in Paganism

We've already touched on some of the issues I feel are holding paganism back and turning it into little more than a fantasy otherworld where we might lose ourselves for an evening or weekend, but here I want to look into them a little more deeply.

As much as paganism is a spiritual system of belief and practice, this hasn't stopped capitalism from turning it into another commodity that can be broken down and sold back to us in the form of crystals, trinkets, incense, and so on. But we also have to realise that hand in hand with capitalism goes consumerism. To some extent we are all guilty of consumerism, because we all exist within the capitalist system. Here I'm talking about mindless consumerism and what I mean by that is when we consume without any thought towards where those products have come from, who was involved with the sourcing and production, nor the harm that may have been caused and the harm they will cause. Mindless consumerism is when we buy this and that because we feel we need it or it makes us feel a certain kind of way. If I'm being honest, then I think we've all probably been guilty of it at some point. We buy something because we think it will add to our spiritual practise but it doesn't take long for the shine to fade and we realise perhaps we didn't really need it in the first place, before we are looking for the next spiritual aide to spend our money on, and so it goes on and on.

I think it's important to say here that I am not against purchasing items that you can't procure or make yourself, or those that genuinely mean something to you. I do think the supporting of crafts people, small shops, publishers, etc. is important, but the mass market of pagan and spiritual goods is rife with tat that add no value whatsoever to anything. You know the kind of stuff I mean: plastic or resin statues and beads, plastic anything for that matter, artificial flowers, crystals and the like. And my biggest bugbear is when this stuff is left in natural and sacred spaces as offerings; for example, nylon ribbons tied to trees. I get that people who leave these things think they are honouring those places and the spirits that reside there, but they aren't. Instead, they are polluting and adding to environmental problems. The *genius loci* do not need these items and in my opinion, it hinders the relationship you might hope to build with them.

Capitalism tries its hardest to persuade us that we need these items for our practises and beliefs, that they are important to us. And we've all felt that temptation and given in to it before. Like I've already said, there is nothing wrong with supporting genuine small businesses like independent crafters, writers, publishers, artists, and bookshops, but we must make a stand against systems that would repackage our beliefs and practises and sell them back to us for profit.

Style over Substance

Aesthetics, as within many other aspects of our lives, holds some importance for us in our spiritualities. Perhaps it is because we humans are visual creatures; much of what we like in life has to do, if only initially, with looks from clothes, homes, and the people we share our lives with. There is absolutely nothing wrong in liking a particular aesthetic when it comes to witchcraft and paganism, but it can be problematic when looks take importance over substance.

Let me be frank, when it comes to practising paganism or witchcraft, looks don't mean shit. By this I don't mean the use of ritual clothing and so on, but instead that folks who don't look like the stereotypical witches or pagans often get sidelined for costume-clad cosplayers without the content or sincerity of their practise ever being considered. My local group consists of a wide variety of people—from nurses to office workers to the unemployed—and when we meet for a moot (a social gathering) you would never guess that the slightly loud group in the corner of the pub hail from various magickal and spiritual traditions.

Oftentimes when new people show an interest and come along to our moot, you see the disappointment on their faces that we are wearing casual everyday clothes and not capes and robes. Often those people never come back, and I must say in some cases that's quite all right! But what it means is that they don't give us a chance based on our looks.

As individuals then, whilst we might enjoy a particular look or trend, it is in no way an indicator of spirituality or commitment for that matter. We can look the part, but if we aren't practising and learning and progressing, then what's the point? Again, this harks back to what we were saying previously about the packaging of our beliefs to be sold back to us. It also means that it is so easy for someone to look the part but have little in terms of actual practise.

Abuse, a Taboo Topic?

Perhaps the biggest and most serious of problems with paganism today is concerned with those people who would seek power over others. Humanity comes in all sorts and varieties, but along with all the good aspects that variety brings there is inevitably the bad; that is, those people who are abusive, narcissistic, and hungry for power over others.

At the least harmful end of the spectrum, we might run into these folks in online groups, and they are usually the type to tell you there's only one right way and it's theirs. They are pretty annoying, but in the confines of an online group quite harmless because we can leave the group and block the person if need be. At worst though, these people run actual covens and groups or organise events. They take advantage of those new to the path and dominate them, perhaps pressuring them into things they don't want to do. Sometimes this can be sexual, especially in coven or group settings where newcomers might be told that they won't be able to progress if they don't perform a sexual ritual. Most of the time, it's about control and power.

You might be thinking that it is easy to avoid such people and groups, but the problem is these people at first can be so charming and friendly. Abusers don't reveal their nefarious selves at first (else people would run a mile to get away from them!) but instead they groom their victims over weeks, months, and even years. And it's not just newcomers to paganism and witchcraft who might find themselves victims of such people. In fact over the last couple of years, some well known figures in the witchcraft community have come forward with their stories of the abuse they've endured. And perhaps the worst part is that once they've stuck their heads above the parapet, after finding the courage to bring their abuse to light, they then endure ridicule, trolling and even more abuse, not only from their abusers but also from their followers or those who think they are lying about their abuse or asking for it, that their treatment was somehow deserved.

Reclaiming witchcraft and paganism means we must stamp out abuse and support those who come forward with their stories. It's important to understand what I am saying here. The role of sex within witchcraft and paganism can be legitimate between partners or where it is consensual between adults who are fully aware of what they are undertaking and want to. But you should never be made to do something against your will or be pressured to do something with the promise of initiation or furthering your role within a group. Trust your gut instinct, for it is very rarely wrong. If something feels wrong to you then it probably is. Get out of there and do not go back.

Reclaiming witchcraft and paganism means we must tear down the structures of capitalism, consumerism, and toxicity. We must burn them to the ground and reclaim those spaces for ourselves which might include creating safe spaces, solidarity, and magickal mutual aid groups. In my opinion, one of the reasons this doesn't occur right now is that we often worry about losing any progress made. Today where it is quite accepted to identify as a pagan or witch, we don't want to endanger this new found credibility and acceptance with the slur of abuse. We've been taught that going back, starting over is somehow a failure but I say otherwise.

Going back to basics, cutting away dead and toxic practises, people, groups, whatever, is the only way we can grow. Sometimes we must go back in order to move forward. The poison must be dug out, no matter how painful, before we can heal. We must become destructive forces, we must embody the energy of The Tower card if we want to build strong and lasting foundations from which rebirth and new growth can emerge.

Individual Reclamation

This reclamation must also occur in our individual practises. The question then is, having rooted out all of the issues we have already covered, what does your practise then become? How do we go about the business of rebuilding something better, something more meaningful?

I've noticed that people don't like to turn the lens inwards and I don't mean that in any kind of negative way, but we feel selfish or stupid for considering our individual needs, for really paying attention to what we really want. Even in individualistic cultures, we're not really individual, the choices we make are often the choices presented to us by societal norms and thus extremely limiting.

For me, this individual reclamation was about stripping everything back to the very basics, getting back to the basis of my beliefs and practise. It was about rediscovering and remembering why and how I came to practise in the first place. It was about rediscovering the magick, the divine, and the connection to it. Everything else came from there. I will share with you how I did this, but remember, this is just my way and yours may look very different. By sharing I hope to inspire you but also to show that it can be done and that the ways are many.

I love hermeticism and for me it explains the universe and our place in it. It was this explanation of the world that helped me to focus on and work on my own individual practise. Here then we will briefly examine the elements and the axis mundi in terms of paganism and witchcraft.

The Elements

We all know that within occult and pagan traditions and theories the elements are important. In many modern practises little but lip service is paid to them or they have places on altars in the set directions because that's what we think we should do, that's what books and others tell us. But why? If it makes no sense to you other than it's the 'norm,' then what is the point?

Going deeper though, the elements in varying degrees and mixations form the whole universe and so some consideration must be given into their placement and their qualities.

Earth: The first of the elements and the most physical, Earth comes first and so it is placed in the north. Earth is the building block of the universe, the clay from which everything is formed. Everything that is solid, that you can touch, hold, and form is of Earth. When in ritual, I hold the Earth in my hand, crumble it between my fingers, smell it. I feel myself seated upon it and notice how it supports me. I understand that my body is Earth, that Earth represents and connects both life and death. It is the final resting place but also the dark of the womb. New beginnings grow from the Earth. It is potential.

Water: Not as physical as Earth but still something we can touch, hold and shape, Water comes next, the second most physical of the elements and so we place it to the left of Earth in the West. Water is fluid, it takes the shape of whatever container it finds itself in. It is adaptable. In ritual, I take a sip of water, hold it in my mouth before swallowing, paying attention to the feel of it. As I do, I consider what Water means, that it represents all liquid. Without it there would be no life. If Earth is the body, then water is the blood. It is the amniotic fluid of pregnancy and birth. It is the sexual secretions of both male and female. It is life.

Air: As we move onto air, the third element, we begin to notice a clear shift in the elements, from the most physical to the least and so this is placed in the East. We can't see or touch air but we know it's there. When we breathe it fills our lungs and we can see how it moves when we watch how it affects other substances, the wind blowing through leaves or how smoke moves on the air currents. In ritual, I breathe deeply, feeling my lungs expand as they fill with air, feeling the movements my body makes to accommodate it. Air carries sound to our ears and scents to our noses. It is inspiration, the winds of change.

Fire: And so we come to the final element, the least physical of the four. It is the opposite of Earth and so we place it in the South. Fire is a plasma. In ritual, I pass my hand over a single candle flame and feel the power of it, the heat of it. Fire is the sun. It is the heat and light that sustains life. It is the spark of animation, the beat of the heart. Our consciousness.

The position of the elements needn't be fixed. Like I said before, what we feel to be true will work best for us and so, for example, if you have a large body of water that lies to the north of your home and dominates your local landscape, you might feel more inclined to place water there instead of to the west. In reclaiming our own individual practises, we must work to gain an understanding of what feels right for us. It's okay to try something and change it if it doesn't work. We must be flexible enough in our approach that we can adapt to new knowledge and information, and incorporate that which aids us. What is important though is that we recognise the elements as the building blocks of the universe and for me that includes the spiritual as well as the physical.

The Axis Mundi

Related to the elements is the concept of the *axis mundi*, the world soul. Many traditions have an understanding of this concept, whether that's Yggdrasil that connects the nine worlds of Norse traditions or the Poteau Mitan, the centre pole of the peristyle within Vodou which the loas descend and ascend, or even the imagery of the World Tree. For now, let's stick with the world tree, as it is an apt metaphor for the soul of the world, that which links all of the realms of existence.

For me, the *axis mundi* has four distinct parts and each relates to one of the elements. If we take our metaphor of a tree then, we see the roots descending into the underworld, anchored in the element of Earth, that element that links death and rebirth. Next we have the lower trunk and it is here that we reside, in the mundane realm. This section is linked to the element of water. Next comes the upper trunk, the celestial realm of the planets, stars, the sun and the moon. This section is linked with the element of Air. And finally we have the branches and leaves, the canopy, the spiritual realm ruled by the element of fire (in many mythologies, fire is a gift from the gods bestowed upon mankind).

When we hold ritual, when we perform workings, we ascend and descend the *axis mundi*, traversing the realms. Any effect we have on one section also affects the others, and so we can see how our individual actions cause ripples throughout all realms. Even when we do not perform ritual or workings, when instead we hope to engage in the spiritual or the divine, we ascend the world tree and the spiritual descends to meet us.

We do not exist in a vacuum. The world is more than we can see, hear, feel, and touch. Understanding this basic notion and putting it into practise—whether you use the analogy of the world tree or your own—is one extremely useful way of stripping back the layers we have accumulated to find the grain of truth at the centre, and it is from here we can build our own individual practises back up to take whatever form fits us best.

The *Genius Loci*

Have you ever felt so connected to a particular place that you just knew the connection was something more, something spiritual? The term *genius loci* means spirit of place, and forming a connection with those spirits where you live can add a deeply spiritual aspect to your individual practise. We may live in a realm dominated by the mundane, but the world is imbued with spirit and connecting with those spirits within our locality needn't be difficult.

When we talk about the *genius loci*, we mean the spirit or spirits in a particular place. These spirits might include spirits of the dead, animal spirits, plant and tree spirits. I believe even places themselves have a spirit or air, that they become imbued with the events that occurred in that place, absorbing the actions and feelings as they accumulate.

As you've progressed through this book you have already begun to build a relationship with the *genius loci*. As you've foraged for food and medicinal plants, you have begun to form connections with those plant spirits. As you have reclaimed the land and sought to protect it, you've grown more connected to the spirits of that land, including the animals that reside there and have formed an alliance with them. You've already done most of the hard work without realising it. Perhaps you've noticed the *genius loci*, maybe you noticed something but didn't know what it was, just that it felt deeper than the mundane, something other. I'm guessing you did, for it is almost impossible to do all you have already done without building an awareness of the spiritual aspect of the land, of places that mean something to you. Now it's just a case of working towards a mindful relationship to the *genius loci*.

In terms of reclamation, working with the *genius loci* can add a liberating aspect to your practise. This relationship isn't dictated by theology or theory, it cannot be repackaged and sold to you nor can anyone tell you what it is supposed to be and it doesn't matter where in the world you are. It is a truly individual relationship determined by how much you are willing to dedicate yourself to it.

There are a number of ways you can increase this relationship and build on the foundations you've already laid. First, continue to get out where you live, continue with those practises you've already begun. Take time to just be in those places without really doing anything. Sit down and watch the world pass. Go out at different times of the day and night and feel the changes that occur in those places, get to really know them, the negative as well as the positive.

I know not everyone is a fan of visualisation or meditation exercises but they can be a great way of connecting with the *genius loci*. This is one I use regularly when I feel I need to. Sometimes it's just to build up the relationship I already have and sometimes I use it to reconnect if I feel the mundane world and all that goes with it has begun to pull me away more than I would like. I include it here for you to use as it is or to change it to fit your own needs however it does need to be done *in situ*.

Go to wherever it is you wish to build your connection to the *genius loci*. Choose somewhere to sit, if there's a tree there then sit so your back is supported by the trunk. Get into a comfortable position. To begin, keep your eyes open. Listen to the sounds around you, the rustle of leaves, birdsong, the buzzing of insects. Let your gaze linger where it will. Watch the interplay of light and shadow.

Feel yourself relaxing. It feels so good to just be and watch the world pass without noticing the passage of time, without caring about it. When you are ready, close your eyes. Take some deep breaths, feeling your chest expand and the movement of your diaphragm. What smells are carried on the air? Allow your breathing to return to normal, and as it does feel the world around you. Feel the tree at your back, the roughness of the bark. Feel the ground as it supports you. Run your hands across its surface, feel the detritus between your fingers.

Listen to the sounds around you, the rustling of leaves, birdsong and buzzing of insects. Notice the shadow and warmth of light behind your closed eyelids. The tree feels solid behind your back. It is supporting you, its roots reaching deep down into the dark earth. Feel yourself connected to the earth, feel yourself rooted to the spot, anchored to this place. Reach your hands up and stretch your fingertips. Reach through the air and towards the sun.

Now relax and just breathe naturally. Listen to the world around you, feel the world around you. Know that you are a part of it, that you are not alone. When you are ready, open your eyes. Let them adjust to the light and let your gaze linger where it will.

You can do this as often as you want. Adjust it to suit yourself in any way you see fit, and remember, the path to reclaiming yourself is your own.

The End

So here we are, at the end of this little book, but before we part ways I just want to say that the path to reclaiming ourselves will not be easy but it's not impossible either. It is my hope that this little book will give you the tools to begin on that journey or at least give you an insight into other ways of being.

I started this book before the panic of COVID-19 took hold of the world, and I finished it whilst in lock down. If there's one thing this virus has shown us it's that we cannot possibly carry on in the same way we always have, and now more people are beginning to wake up to this fact, people who before would have been more than happy to continue with the status quo.

If this book helps us to live a little freer, if it sparks a little something inside of you, dear reader, then I will consider it a massive success, after all, revolution begins not with a flood, but with a trickle and so let this add to your flow. Let us reclaim ourselves for I fear no one will do it for us.

Resist beautifully, people.

Emma Kathryn

Emma Kathryn lives in the middle of England in a small rural town. A long time animist, witch and obeah woman, Emma truly believes we have the power and the tools to reclaim the world, making it that which we wish it to be. She writes for Gods & Radicals, practises witchcraft, reads tarot and can be found roaming woodlands whenever she gets the chance.

Gods&Radicals Press

Founded in 2015, Gods&Radicals Press is a not-for-profit Pagan anti-capitalist publisher with over 20 titles published to date. For more information, visit our website at ABEAUTIFULRESISTANCE.ORG